# What Keeps You Awake At Night?

**Creating Financial Security**

**Without Unnecessary Risk, Fees or Exposure**

Author:

Frank R. Riedel IV

Hope you enjoy the Book!

Frank Riddle

WHAT KEEPS YOU AWAKE AT NIGHT?

WHAT KEEPS YOU AWAKE AT NIGHT?

ISBN 9781079802450

Independently Published in the USA.

WHAT KEEPS YOU AWAKE AT NIGHT?

# 4
## WHAT KEEPS YOU AWAKE AT NIGHT?

# Dedication and Acknowledgments

It is with great appreciation that I would like to dedicate this book and to thank those people who have made such large contributions to my life and career. First, to the families and individuals that I have had the pleasure to work with in my career over many years. I cannot thank you enough for your trust and confidence in me.

To Michael & Jennifer Avery for always having my back, thank you. To many Colleagues over the years. To name a few, a special thank you to Bruce Stedwell for your friendship, hard work and sheer determination. It has been a pleasure to see how you have developed. To Eric Kouvolo for your hard work in this industry and your friendship and for writing the forward for this book. You are a true credit to our industry. To Bill Walton for your friendship and for always believing in me. To Robert Newhart for your friendship, support and honesty and integrity. To Justin & Shannon Ross for your friendship and support. To Bobby Hancock for your friendship & advice. To Steve Pataki, I greatly value your friendship.

On a more personal note, I'd like to dedicate this book to my late parents Frank & Irene Riedel for making my life largely what it is today. I would also like to dedicate this to my siblings Irene, Dennis, Becky, Linda, my niece Katie & nephew Mike for the roles that each of you have played in my life. To Deb Hilton for your kindness. Thank you, Nicole Ball for always making me look good for my publicity photos.

Last, but not least, a Special Thank You to my Beautiful Wife Angela for your Love, Support and for your Consistent Encouragement.

**6**
WHAT KEEPS YOU AWAKE AT NIGHT?

# Table of Contents

WHAT KEEPS YOU AWAKE AT NIGHT?

**8**
WHAT KEEPS YOU AWAKE AT NIGHT?

# Foreword

I've never been a believer in luck. The Roman philosopher Seneca once said, "Luck is what happens when preparation meets opportunity." I met Mr. Frank Riedel of Hurricane Financial nearly a decade ago. Today, I feel honored to write this foreword.

There were two books that made a profound change in the way I think about work and wealth. The combined philosophies of these books are what lead me on a quest where I found Mr. Riedel. Quickly, I discovered his deep knowledge of both subjects and knew that I had found an intellectual goldmine.

Through my interactions with Hurricane Financial, Frank proved to be an expert in his field. Many other "advisors" lacked the extensive knowledge of the products they were promoting, and I realized that there was a real difference between a true professional and a salesperson.

Most other advisors were also missing something I consider essential: PASSION. You can tell when someone truly believes in what they say. Frank exudes enthusiasm while helping his clients achieve peace of mind with their finances. I also recognized two other principles that were uncommon in our industry: Integrity and Vision. Many "advisors" will recommend a product just to make a commission or charge management fees. Frank is a great example of a professional who performs as a true fiduciary for his clients.

Through the years, I realized the mistakes I had previously made

**9**

before learning the concepts in this book. Not just little mistakes. After crunching the numbers, I realized that I had thrown away over One MILLION Dollars in opportunity cost! Most Americans are unknowingly and unwillingly making the same mistakes. I wish I had met Frank 10 years sooner.

This book will challenge many previously held beliefs about growing, protecting and preserving your wealth. It is without doubt, that the knowledge and principles contained within these pages, can help you avoid those common mistakes and to create a solid foundation for your retirement!

Eric Kouvolo
Founder, The Wealth Foundation

# About the Author:

**Frank Riedel IV** is the President and Founder of Hurricane Financial Corporation, a company dedicated to bettering the financial lives of their clients and their client's families.

Mr. Riedel is a Certified Estate Planner®, Wealth Strategist, Retirement Income Strategist, and Infinite Banking Concept® Authorized Practitioner. Fusing time-tested wealth building principles with personalized advice; Frank enjoys helping people become better educated in the areas of strategic wealth planning and retirement income planning. Frank works with clients in many states from coast to coast in various life stages. Widely considered an expert in areas such as Retirement Income Planning, Strategic Wealth Planning as well as other areas within the industry, Frank has also mentored and trained many financial professionals on these subjects over the years.

A Native of Southern California, Frank now resides with his wife of 20+ years Angela in Beautiful North Carolina. He enjoys spending quality time with family and friends. As a Christian, Frank's faith provides a compass as to how he conducts his business and interacts with his clients.

Ephesians 2:10 (NIV)

[10] For we are God's handiwork, created in Christ Jesus to do good works, which God prepared in advance for us to do.

WHAT KEEPS YOU AWAKE AT NIGHT?

**12**
WHAT KEEPS YOU AWAKE AT NIGHT?

# Preface

I have worked with clients from many different backgrounds and that experience has ultimately led me to write this book. Too often people end up placing their financial future in someone else's hands by simply finding an advisor who looks good in a suit and talks "the language". Taking time to research strategies, concepts and options is always your best course of action without risking the very thing that you are trying to grow and protect.

As far back as I can remember, I can recall being concerned about just about everything that seemed out of my control. One day as a young child I came inside the house to grab a bite to eat and overheard my parents having a "conversation" about finances. Even at that young age I wanted to help any way I could. I guess the need to feel secure is in us all even as children. I remember my father saying to me in that moment, "Frank, this isn't anything that you need to concern yourself with. You'll have plenty of time when you're older to concern yourself over adult things like money and important decisions. Just go back out and play with your friends and enjoy being young while you still are." However, at that young age I failed to grasp the importance of what my father was trying to tell me until some years later. It's amazing how smart your parents look as you get older.

One day you look up and you are an adult. By the way, that's *"code"* for someone with an insane amount of obligations, pressures and responsibilities. Career, Family, Finances just to name a few. With today's fast paced lifestyle in mind, it's easy to see how proper retirement planning is often placed on the back burner.

WHAT KEEPS YOU AWAKE AT NIGHT?

As you read this book, I encourage you to continue to learn and ask a lot of questions. The strategies outlined in this book such as The Banking Policy Strategy™ have personally changed my life and the lives of countless clients, family and friends. Likewise, the idea of Guaranteed Lifetime Income is so critical especially as you age. Having the peace of mind that Guaranteed Lifetime Income brings is something that cannot be measured.

This book is intended to offer up ideas and concepts and to stimulate thought and reflection. We will discuss proven wealth accumulation and wealth preservation strategies that are commonly misrepresented or misunderstood by many people as well as many financial professionals.

Frank Riedel IV

# Chapter One

## The Challenge We All Face

It is said that everyone experiences "The Day" when you are standing in front of a mirror and just at that moment you realize that you are starting to get older. This happens to all of us at some point. For some, it is realized earlier than for others. This realization can set off a domino effect in any number of areas in your life. Sometimes people begin asking themselves many questions, often-times in the middle of the night when you're trying unsuccessfully to turn off your thoughts and sleep. Questions like...

*"When should I retire?"*

*"Will I run out of money when I'm retired?"*

*"What will my Legacy be when I'm gone?"*

Putting together a strategic retirement plan is similar to what you often see in the health and fitness industry. Most fitness related tv commercials start by restating the prevailing feeling of most people, "I just don't have enough time in my day to join a gym or begin some tedious diet. This is typically followed up by the introduction of the next *"life changing"* piece of fitness equipment. You are led to imagine that in just 10 minutes a week you too can look like the model featured in the commercial. Chances are you know the types of equipment I'm referring to. The same pieces of equipment that end up in the attic or the garage until the day that your spouse or someone else *"encourages"* you to put that piece of equipment out of its misery and out it goes! The problem isn't usually a lack of time. The problem usually stems from a lack of desire to eat right and exercise. Unfortunately, a lot of people treat proper retirement planning the same way.

## The Monster Under the Bed!

Studies have shown that more than ½ of the population is concerned about outliving their finances. Being fiscally proactive along the way while still balancing all that life can throw at us on a regular basis is challenging. Over time, the lack of attention to your retirement plans can lead to a sense of dread when you realize it is time to get serious and start to face the monster. Allow me to paint a picture for illustration purposes. You might have normal, typical childhood memories of things like *The Monster Under the Bed.* This can be brought on by something as simple as what you saw on tv that scared you. I can recall as a child and looking under my bed not once but twice before turning the light off. This feeling can make it difficult to sleep. As an adult, the feeling can be just as powerful. The only difference is that now the "monster" is a great big, ominous cloud of stress brought on by fear of the unknown and questions about the future.

Adding to the stress of it all is the seemingly unending flow of information and advertising that is targeting you. If you are of a certain age demographic you are in the crosshairs. Think about it, seemingly every time you go to the mailbox there is a seminar invitation. You cannot watch a sporting event without usually seeing several well-placed ads from financial companies. By the way, they do know how to pick very friendly, honest and knowledgeable looking actors to portray advisors. The underlying fear of the unknown especially as it relates to your retirement can become the scariest monster of them all. This is what keeps a lot of hard-working adults awake at night. Does this sound familiar?

At this point I would challenge you to take a moment, turn down the "noise" around you and simply hear this. "You do Not need to risk your

WHAT KEEPS YOU AWAKE AT NIGHT?

financial future to achieve your financial goals and dreams." It starts with little bit of education and honest reflection along with the willingness to consider all options. The peace and confidence that comes from knowing that your retirement is secure can be a powerful sleep aid.

*"Most people don't plan to fail;*

*they fail to plan"* - John L. Beckley

### Will I Run Out Of Money In Retirement?

Now that is The Question! Unless your relationship with your children is so great that both you and your children look forward to the day that you move in with them, making sure you have enough money in your later years is an important key. Quite possibly, THE KEY.

**Life Expectancies in 1970**

**Men 67 Years, Women 75 Years.**

**Life Expectancies in 2020**

**Men 77 Years, Women 82 Years**

WHAT KEEPS YOU AWAKE AT NIGHT?

According to these estimates, in just a 50 Year period Men's age jumped by 10 years on average. Women' average age jumped by 7 years. That's good news on one hand and cause for concern on the other. I recently read that an estimated 1/2 to 2/3 of people are concerned about running out of money in retirement. I'm sure that there are a number of people reading this book that are already feel very secure and the fear of …I meant, the joy of moving in with family later in life doesn't apply. The flipside of that is that **if you're not feeling 100% certain that your money will last the remainder of your lifetime, you may want to keep an open mind at this point as you continue reading.**

Common advice and opinions will tell you that you can never make up for lost years. You might also hear that you need to have a very large retirement nest egg to guarantee that you'll have enough money in your retirement. The internet is filled with helpful calculator tools. Many of these "tools" are simply designed to get you to click on some financial company's website or info capture page. The goal is a simple one and the tools are strategically designed to persuade you into the corral with the rest of the herd. Case in point, Joe annuity salesman. Annuities can be an excellent way to protect your retirement income from unnecessary risk and exposure…if you know what fees are involved.

Fees will destroy growth faster than almost anything else. Today, if you are considering an annuity there are a great number of choices out there as well as a great number of salesmen. Too often people buy annuities and other financial products like snacks from a vending machine. When people purchase a snack from a vending machine it comes down to taste. Almost

WHAT KEEPS YOU AWAKE AT NIGHT?

no one reads the back of the packaging before making their selection. Knowing what is contained within might cause you to make a better decision. Financial products are very similar. Fees, like unwanted calories, add up quickly!

## THE TRUTH.

Too many people have mistakenly bought in to the misconception that fees are just part of the game and that risk tolerance is the determining factor in making potentially bigger earnings. Despite common opinions, you can secure your retirement against losses while still earning gains. What's more, it can be accomplished without risking your future or paying astronomical fees along the way. Just as an example, do you have an IRA or previous or current 401K? Depending upon your own personal scenario, it might be wise to consider protecting a percentage of your hard-earned nest egg. Building out a Strategic Income Plan could provide valuable peace of mind when it comes to your retirement. In the upcoming chapters we will dive into time-tested methods of Wealth Accumulation, Wealth Preservation and Retirement Income Planning that are Proven, Safe Strategies but often widely misrepresented by a lot of industry professionals. When you learn how to eliminate the unknown and unnecessary risk of loss while also eliminating or at least greatly reducing fees and tax consequences, you may find that you are already a lot closer to your goals than you had previously thought.

WHAT KEEPS YOU AWAKE AT NIGHT?

Ask yourself this question, "If you set out on a journey to somewhere and you were going the wrong direction how soon would you want to know?" Long before a crew member on The RMS Titanic uttered the words *"Iceberg, straight ahead"* the passengers and crew of that vessel were already, unknowingly on a course for disaster. New information along with navigational adjustments would have allowed for better decisions to be made thus avoiding disaster.

## Accumulation vs Preservation

There are typically two major points of emphasis within the financial community which override all others. Accumulation and Preservation. The common thought is that when you are younger and gainfully employed, you are in accumulation mode. The accumulation mode is often based upon risk tolerance. This isn't always the case; however, a lot of advisors believe that younger people should be more aggressive simply because they are young and the need to accumulate is great. When you are older and nearing retirement, you are in preservation mode. The preservation mode is usually thought of as a conservative approach with less risk. That sounds simple but like the passengers on that great ship crossing the Northern Atlantic over one hundred years ago, a great number of people today are on a financial course that all too often has a sad ending. Better information provides for better decisions thus avoiding hidden *financial icebergs.*

Recently I met with a new client in my office. I wish that I could say that this case was uncommon but it's actually very common today. For the purposes of this book let's just refer to the client as George. During our initial face to face meeting, George and I discussed in some detail where he was in life and what goals were most important to him. Sadly, I discovered that his wife of many years passed away recently. George was also quick to point out that being a person in his late 60's, he was risk adverse. At this stage of George's life, he had two simple yet important goals.

## Number One: Protect his hard-earned retirement accounts from unexpected losses.

## Number Two: Creating of a Legacy for future generations of his family.

George had worked and retired from a company where he had been employed for over 35 years. He also indicated that over his lifetime, he had always been viewed as a saver. Unlike a lot of people today George and his late wife lived a very comfortable but simple lifestyle while working and raising their family even though they had financial resources that many others did not have. As we concluded our initial meeting, I asked George if he had worked with any advisor or estate planner at any point recently. George looked directly at me and said, "that's why I'm here." He

WHAT KEEPS YOU AWAKE AT NIGHT?

went on to tell me that he felt like his recent advisor was failing to truly listen to him. I asked George to gather up his financial statements and insurance documents and we scheduled our follow up meeting at my office.

One week later and 10 minutes early George arrived at my office for our 2$^{nd}$ meeting. This time he was fully armed with financial and insurance related statements as well as spreadsheets which he had created, etc. After looking over his information one thing was as clear as anything. For a person who considers himself a conservative investor, he had 90% of his portfolio at risk and not only that but what most would conclude as high risk. George told me that he felt uneasy with the markets, the economy and other more politically related topics. I couldn't help but to ask him how often he had previously met with his advisor to discuss topics such as strategy or allocation. George said that his now, previous advisor didn't talk all that often and that the advisor told him that he was doing fine and then shifted the conversation towards other topics such as golf. The funny part is that George is not a golfer as he went on to say. If George had been my first new client, I might have found this scenario surprising. But over the years I have worked with many different types of people and I see and hear this sort of thing regularly. It is what I refer to as the auto-pilot advisor. Often, I see people like George in aggressive accumulation products versus a Personalized Accumulation and/or Guaranteed Preservation Strategies. Over the following days I was able to build-out a Guaranteed Lifetime Income Plan for George and helped him transition his hard-earned assets to a Strategy of Protection and Guarantees. In addition to helping George secure a guaranteed lifetime stream, he left my

WHAT KEEPS YOU AWAKE AT NIGHT?

office with the peace of mind that his estate and legacy were in order and assurance that future generations of his family would benefit as a result.

In summary, **the very things that benefitted you in your earlier stages of life are often the same things that will destroy your finances and cause stress and tension in your later stages of life.** Optimism can be good but just don't allow mere hope to be your strategy!

WHAT KEEPS YOU AWAKE AT NIGHT?

# Chapter Two

## Herd Mentality

If you've ever witnessed a herd migration in person or watched an old western movie you might better appreciate what I'm about to say. One of the staples of old western films is the drama and excitement of "the drive." Against all odds, a cowboy successfully brings in a large group of steers to market. Have you ever wondered just what captivates people so much about a period in history such as the wild west days? Many things would be the answer. But if you long to experience days gone by and the thrill of the unknown cheer up, many of the thrills that our great, great grandparents experienced in their time are still able to be seen today if you know where to look. Don't believe it? Allow me to illustrate the driving of the herd as just one example. Today marketing companies and consumer research companies have successfully moved large groups of people for years. Centuries ago large groups of people could be moved or influenced through sheer intimidation or fear. Later it was the published word, newsprint, etc. Radio came along and reached into people's homes. Television then became the way to control the masses. The Internet opened people up to the Information Superhighway. And on and on it goes. The greatest display of "herding" is actually taking place right now. Cowboy hats and brands are being replaced by profiling data and large-scale marketing budgets. We are told what to eat, what to wear, how we should

WHAT KEEPS YOU AWAKE AT NIGHT?

look, how we should feel and every few years, how to vote. Market research shows that people most often make impulsive and emotional decisions. Making these sorts of decisions in financial matters can cripple your retirement and reduce your golden years to something far less than what you had ever imagined.

## Lesson of the Bison!

Bison are a classic example. It only takes a couple to start moving and a chaos ensues. The next thing you know it's an entire herd stampeding along. When the markets and our economy is going well our media sources tell us we should be invested or miss out on the opportunity. When markets and economic factors are not so good our sources of media usually offer up the opposing viewpoint. Most people would admit to feeling confused and even discouraged at times. The result of this is what leads many people to make important financial decisions in a reactive state versus a proactive state. Take the time to explore options. It is equally important to be sure that your strategy lines up with your stage of life. There's a great deal of people out there who are in strategies that would be better suited for someone in an earlier stage of life instead of someone approaching retirement or already retired. The lesson of the bison is simply this, **making quick, reactive decisions can have dangerous consequences.**

## The Dinner Seminar Invitation

Recently, I noticed a rather large number of direct mail pieces being delivered to my mailbox. Yes, I am referring to The Financial Dinner Seminar Invitation.  I'm not a huge fan of junk mail so I typically discard and recycle these types of mail pieces somewhat quickly. I discovered a few weeks later that several of my neighbors had also been targeted in this recent *Herding Attempt*…I meant mail campaign.

WHAT KEEPS YOU AWAKE AT NIGHT?

One of my neighbors, let's just refer to him as John, told me that he goes to as many dinner seminars as he can. As it turns out, John loves steak dinners! If the invite mentions a good local steakhouse, John is in. Being inquiry natured, I had to ask a question or two. I asked him if the information seemed to be worthwhile? his reply was No. He didn't get much out of it. I asked if he had sat down with the advisor for a follow up meeting yet. As it turns out, caller ID was making it possible for John to avoid any follow up meetings or pressure to meet with anyone. To me at least, it seems like a lot to go through for a free meal but tens of thousands do this every week across the United States.

As a professional working in this industry for as long as I have, I already knew the answers to the questions that I had asked my neighbor before I had even asked. I simply wanted to hear the response from the other side of the literal fence. Over the years I have had just about every marking firm out there contact me about doing seminars. It is amazing to say the least what top marketing companies know about YOU. This may come as a shock to some readers, but dinner invitations are not just randomly mailed out. In reality it is quite the opposite. Top marketing firms know your age range, income range and approximate net worth. Putting you firmly in the crosshairs of any financial firm that uses the marketing company's services. Typically, you register via a webpage or information capture page. This step is critical to the financial company. This step allows for you to knowingly and willingly give over your personal contact info. Step one has now been implemented. Next comes the dinner presentation. This is scripted and rehearsed again and again, until it sounds convincing enough. Step two is now completed. Next is the

WHAT KEEPS YOU AWAKE AT NIGHT?

follow up office visit. In most cases this is where you'll see the advisor's smiling face and possibly even a new suit or tie. All designed to impress you. This concludes step three. From there, you'll find yourself at a pivotal fork in the road. Feeling overwhelmed at this point is the reason too many people settle for a smiling face. Someone who looks good in a suit. Someone who sounds knowledgeable. It's just a lot easier to let someone else handle all of this financial responsibility.

It is equally as Important to understand **Assets Under Management. AUM**, as it is known by in the financial industry is unfortunately what a lot of licensed advisors use as a measuring rod for their business. I had lunch with a financial advisor recently whom I have known for some time. Lunch began with the customary small talk. Soon thereafter the conversation turned to business. I asked my lunch companion how business was treating him. I expected to hear how the practice was growing and maybe something about how after 15 years, what a privilege it was to be a trusted advisor to so many people. Maybe I hoped for too much. What I got back in response was 12 straight minutes of AUM talk. It was Total AUM. Then Target AUM and Projected AUM. The waiter returned a third time to try to take our orders and the AUM monologue was still being heard. We finally did get to order but by then my appetite wasn't what it was prior. Why was AUM so important to that advisor? Simple, the advisor had planned to build up his book of business to an AUM dollar amount, then eventually sell the business and ride off into the sunset. Hawaii to be exact. On the way out of the restaurant he invited me to "take a peek" at his new Mercedes. It was nice! I have no issue with a hard-working advisor earning a great income and having a nice lifestyle.

However, the lunch conversation left me to wonder whose retirement was he more focused on, his clients or his own?

I'm not trying to be too critical of advisors or marketing approaches. There are some genuine, good, honest and talented advisors out there. However, there are more product selling salespeople than most consumers are aware of. **Taking time to really weigh options and advice is critical**.

Today, marketing companies are now trying to pedal the seminar idea as some sort of a workshop. I've conducted a workshop or two in my time. Simply calling a dinner seminar a workshop doesn't automatically make it so. Here's one tip that can help to determine the difference. *If there is a Steak Dinner on the menu, it's not a workshop. It's a seminar.*

## The Big Company Advisor Dilemma.

WHAT KEEPS YOU AWAKE AT NIGHT?

Too often people simply give in to the perceived comfort security of the big company name. It's easy to see why as financial advertising is everywhere. I kept track during one college football game that I watched on tv and I counted 12 such ads. That's at least 3 per quarter. All the ads had one thing in common. A warm, trustworthy face to greet them. The background music was well placed too. It was on the level of most Hollywood films. The only difference was this *"film"* was only 30-60 seconds or so long, but the acting was top notch!

I spoke with a couple recently about their retirement plan and inquired as to how they had landed with the large national financial firm that they had been with before speaking with me. The couple turned and looked at each other for a few seconds and then the husband said, they sold us on their name and size. This is one of the biggest stumbling blocks for many people. The issue is not the company size. It is not the assets under management. It is not the years of experience. The issue comes down to the client's best interest.

One critical point that I wanted to help this couple to understand was the difference between **Captive vs Independent Companies and Captive vs Independent Advice.** In most, if not all cases, when you become a client of the large national company you are receiving advice from a captive advisor. If you are getting your financial advice from a wealth manager at a bank you are working with a captive advisor. *What is a Captive Company or Advisor?* Being "Captive" means that the advisor can only offer products and services that his company provides to their clientele. Picture it this way. What if you were looking to purchase a home and signed on with a real estate company and that the realtor whom you

WHAT KEEPS YOU AWAKE AT NIGHT?

were working with ONLY showed you homes listed by their company? That would certainly cause me to find another company and realtor. With that being said, I'm amazed sometimes as to why investors never make that connection. While I want to believe that a captive advisor truly wishes to help their clients, it's hard to see how they can be truly objective without violating their employment agreement.

This point leads to another one. What if your current advisor was a captive advisor and you asked your advisor for his or her opinion on an "Outside" product, strategy or idea? I think you can picture his or her reaction for yourself. There is an industry expression called *"kill it and redirect."* This is simply the response or tactic taught by most firms. First the advisor tells you that outside product, strategy or idea is not something that he or she would recommend. Of course, they wouldn't recommend it. Hello! They can't recommend it. They are captive to their employment agreement. When they've succeeded in *killing it* and making you feel silly for even considering outside, independent advice, they will then *redirect* you back to the menu of products and services that they as captives, can offer. Talk about a Conflict of Interest!

Meanwhile, Independent Companies and Advisors may not have a multi-billion-dollar ad campaign working for them 24/7 but Independent Financial Professionals have the ability to offer truly unbiased advice and products and services from every corner of the financial services and insurance industries. But regardless of which path you take, Captive or Independent, **find an advisor who truly listens to you and puts your objectives above their own**.

WHAT KEEPS YOU AWAKE AT NIGHT?

# A Brief Look at Economic Historical Events

Whether you are an optimistic type or a bit more pessimistic, those who understand history can usually agree on one thing. Nobody can truly predict the future. Especially as it relates to Complex Global Economics. I for one, am not a risk taker when it comes to my money or that of my clients. However, I cannot help but to notice patterns that continually astonish me. A good example would be the last couple of market crashes.

My clients are protected against risk and market declines are not much of a concern. Because of my curiosity, I cannot stop consuming economic data. What the data says to me is that when the markets suffer significant destructive losses, people in large part tend to disavow the markets and look for better financial options to grow their wealth. But there is an old saying, *Time Heals All Wounds*. At some point, enough time has passed by and those same people whom may have disavowed the markets a couple years earlier are now, like The Bison, stampeding back once again to the very edge of the financial cliff. Why does this pattern tragically repeat itself again and again? There are many, many theories. I believe it's just simply (FOMO) *Fear Of Missing Out*. It really doesn't take much for the stampede to start. For example, one of the major news networks invites a Pro-Market type of person to be a guest on their network and it begins. Invariably the guest will drone on and on about how such events like an improving jobs report or GDP or the newly Elected DC Political Structure is boosting the markets and how *"The Smart Money"* is getting back into the markets at a record pace. Or something along those lines. If you listen

WHAT KEEPS YOU AWAKE AT NIGHT?

closely at this point you can begin to hear the early, first steps of the herd beginning to rumble. The next thing you know we're completely inundated by Internet, TV, Radio and Prints ads urging *"The Smart Investors"* to abandon all common sense…and ultimately leading you to contact XYZ Mega Firm and meet with an advisor today.

Historically speaking, financial markets the world over have seen good years and bad years. Major financial turmoil can be traced back as far as the 1600's.

**Dutch Tulip Crash** in the late 1630's caused the Dutch economy such devastation that it took years to recover from. Many people became unemployed and destitute.

The United States has been no stranger to the devastating effects of market turmoil. While there was plenty of Financial Turmoil prior to 1900, let's focus on the $20^{th}$ and $21^{st}$ Centuries.

**The Stock Market Crash of 1929**. By the beginning of the $4^{th}$ quarter of 1929 the markets imploded and sent the US economy into the stuff of nightmares. Over 25 Billion Dollars were lost almost overnight. Banks began shutting down. Nearly 140 Billion Dollars in accounts evaporated seemingly overnight. Over 80 Million Dollars in personal savings were lost. The crash of 1929 has spawned many books and movies over the years. Gone was the roar of the Roaring 20's. Cocktail parties started to be replaced by soup lines. Very high unemployment became the new normal.

WHAT KEEPS YOU AWAKE AT NIGHT?

It took 12+ years to recover from the crash of 1929 aka Black Monday. Some would argue that they themselves never fully recovered.

**The 1946 – 1947 Post War Effect.** The DOW dropped 23% as post war demand dropped sharply. This triggered high unemployment and low economic confidence.

**The DOW drop of 27%+ December 1961 - June 1962.** Fueled by Cold War fears, The Cuban Missile Crisis and US labor issues.

**US Political Turmoil December 1968 – May 1970**. On the heels of a sharp 25% DOW decline in 1966, civil unrest, high inflation, race riots became major news events in 1968. The DOW declined once again. This time by 35%

**Arab Oil Embargo, Watergate Crisis 1973 – 1974**. The Oil Embargo triggered another US Financial Flashpoint. Long, Long Lines at the gas pump and painfully high prices for fuel. The Watergate Scandal forced President Nixon to resign. The DOW declined 45%.

**Souring Interest Rates, Stagflation 1980 – 1982**. The Fed pushed interest rates to the 20% range. All of this triggered painfully slow growth and a DOW decline of 24%.

**The Stock Market Crash of 1987**. This event was the largest single day crash in US history. The market lost 23% and once again, hard-working Americans were hit extremely hard.

**The 1999 – 2000 Dot.com Bubble Bursts**. For several years leading up to 1999, technology was the new shiny toy that seemingly everyone

WHAT KEEPS YOU AWAKE AT NIGHT?

wanted to invest in. What could possibly go wrong? Widespread speculation ensued. Once again, many hard-working Americans found that their retirement to now be put off a while.

**The Economic Crash 2008 – October 2007 – March 2009.** Easy credit money in 2006 and 2007 started to come to a head in late 2007 – 2008. The housing/mortgage crisis was now here. Mortgage giant Countrywide went out of business. Wall Street giants such as Bear Stearns & Lehman Brothers were toppled. The DOW declined 53%. Millions of hard-working Americans found their retirement accounts devastated. The devastating effects would last for years to come.

The history of the markets is a tumultuous one. Fortunes have been made and far too often fortunes have been lost. History tells a sad story of Americans being all too caught up in a get rich quick, buy now pay later mindset.

**No one can predict when the next "big" downturn will be, but one thing history has shown us is for sure…there will be another devasting market downturn. Are you prepared?**

Sources: CNBC.com, History.com, The Street.com, Investment News, The Smithsonian Channel.

WHAT KEEPS YOU AWAKE AT NIGHT?

*"Those who don't know history are doomed to repeat it." — Edmund Burke*

In the next chapter we will look at **The Rate of Return Myth & The Dark Side of Compound Interest.** I will illustrate how compound interest can work against you just as much or more. In later chapters, we will take a detailed look into **The Power of Zero.** We will also explore strategies that can help you **Eliminate Unnecessary Risk and Fees.**

WHAT KEEPS YOU AWAKE AT NIGHT?

# The Sad Impact of the 401(K)

You may have a current or old 401(k) today but most are unfamiliar with its origins. In 1978 Congress passed the Revenue Act. This Act included Section 401(k). The law went into full effect on January 1, 1980. A 401(k) is simply a retirement savings plan that is sponsored by an employer. The plan allows employees of the sponsoring employer to invest portions of their paychecks to a retirement account and taxes are deferred until distributions are taken. This typically happens once the employee is fully retired and over 59 ½ years old. Penalties occur on distributions prior to age 59 ½. Widespread plan participation kicked into high gear in the early 1980's. Employees were now allowed to contribute using payroll deductions, the 401(k) was off to the races and the retirement landscape would never be the same. By 1983 nearly half of all large companies were sponsoring a 401(k). There was in excess of $384 Billion Dollars in 401(k) accounts with over 19 million active participants by 1990. 401(k) assets climbed north of $1 Trillion Dollars with over 30 million active participants by 1996. By 2017 401(k) Plans totaled $4.8 Trillion plus.

Most plan proponents, historians and economist agree that the 401(k) plan wasn't originally proposed as a primary mode of retirement saving. **The bottom line is that the advent of the 401(k) gave Employers a Much Cheaper, Easier way to offer a retirement account to their employees than what it would cost to fund a Pension Account. The shift from pension accounts to the 401(k) effectively transferred the**

WHAT KEEPS YOU AWAKE AT NIGHT?

**Risk and Responsibility from the employer to the individual employee. This shift also exposed investors to conflicting advice when working with members of financial services industry.**

Today, most people have mixed feelings or a skewed view of the Historical Performance of their 401(k). Because so many Baby Boomers were gainfully employed and had invested in their 401(k) in the 1980's and 1990's, many benefitted from the Bull Markets of that period. Since that time, we've witnessed historical highs and historical lows. Some people are actually surprised and upset when their 401(k) accounts suffer a significant loss. Are you kidding? This is what can happen when you **Gamble on Your Financial Future!** How quickly people are willing to forget the anguish and devastation of the 2008 crash or previous crashes.

I've heard various starry eyed 401(k) supporting, asset under management financial advisors, attempt to counter the argument by simply saying *"yeah but if you stayed in long-term, you made it all back."* That argument is possibly the stupidest argument ever stated! A person must also factor in lost time, and the cost of the loss of opportunity. Not to mention fees continuing to be paid along the way. You see, simply getting back what you lost isn't good enough. See: The Late Great Rate of Return Myth illustrated in Chapter 3. **How about not losing any money whatsoever while building wealth for the future? Now there is a thought!**

Sources: CNBC.com, Nasdaq.com, Investopedia.com, Barrons.com, Politico.com

WHAT KEEPS YOU AWAKE AT NIGHT?

**40**
WHAT KEEPS YOU AWAKE AT NIGHT?

# Chapter Three

## The Wall Street Casino – Place Your Bets!

If you've ever passed through a casino you can probably relate to this. Casinos are designed to make entrance easy. Finding the door out takes much more effort. As you've most certainly guessed by now, I am no gambler. Frequenting casinos is not something I'm familiar with. But a few years back I had to attend a business conference in Las Vegas. The conference was held at a big-name hotel along the Famous Vegas Strip. In between meetings I had a chance to pass through the casino floor area one evening. As I strolled through the thick layer of smoke, mirrors, lights and noise, I noticed people from all demographics were well represented in that place. I cannot see why some people get caught up in this. I thought as I navigated my way through it all and finally located an exit, "It is clear to see why in life, so many people lose, while so few people win". Las Vegas will likely always be a destination city but with the advent of industries such as fantasy sports, internet wagering and favorable legislation, gambling is everywhere now, and it appears to be here to stay. But make no mistake about it, *Legalized Gambling* has been available from coast to coast for over a century. AKA Wall Street. Over the last century Americans have adopted an appetite for financial thrill seeking.

## The Baby Boomer Effect

The generation who came through the Great Depression of the 1930's and a generation or two that followed them had a very different view. The painful effects of the Great Depression were still fresh. All you had to do was to talk to your parents or grandparents and you were reminded of tales of financial hardship. People valued hard work and enterprise back then. Risk was not a popular strategy. But years pass by and babies were born, older people passed away. In the process…mindsets began to change. Today, most Americans find themselves caught up in a *"Me First, Got to Have It Now"* mindset. This is all somewhat understandable and so very predictable. Let's take **The Baby Boomer Generation** for example. Baby Boomers are defined as Americans born between 1946 – 1964.

WHAT KEEPS YOU AWAKE AT NIGHT?

The internet is filled with data on The Baby Boomer Generation. Most estimates say that there are currently approximately 76 Million Boomers out there. The makes up Approximately 29% of The US population. The first group of Boomers became the "retirement Age 65" in 2011. Now when you consider a demographic the size of The Baby Boomers and the fact that people are living longer today than in decades past you can see why the fear of running out of money is a very real concern. I would liken it to a basketball going through a garden hose. At some point, those retirees will need to start living-off of what they've managed to save over their lives.

In the coming years we will witness The Largest Transfer of Wealth Ever! Since we know that baby boomers and the advent of the 401(k) boosted market growth. **Ask yourself the question,** *when that baby boomer bulge finally makes its way through the hose completely, what then? How do The Markets replace that money?*

WHAT KEEPS YOU AWAKE AT NIGHT?

# The Dark Side of Compound Interest

Understanding how an average rate of return can be misleading is a good start. Now let's look at an example of *The Dark Side of Compound Interest* and its effects on your investments.

**10% Lost**

**11% Needed to Break Even**

**20% Lost**

**25% Needed to Break Even**

The number one thing that most people fail to understand about losses is the amount of gain and time needed just to get back to where you once were. The chart above illustrates this fact. If you lost 10%, it will take 11% in gain to recoup the initial loss of 10%. If you lost 20% it's a lot worse. You'll need 25% in gain just to recoup the loss of 20%.

```
 ╭───────────────────────────╮
 │        40% Lost           │
 ╰───────────────────────────╯

 ╭───────────────────────────╮
 │       67% Needed          │
 │     to Break Even         │
 ╰───────────────────────────╯
```

If you lost 40%, it will take a whopping 67% in gain to recoup the loss of 40%.

```
 ╭───────────────────────────╮
 │        50% Lost           │
 ╰───────────────────────────╯

 ╭───────────────────────────╮
 │      100% Needed          │
 │     to Break Even         │
 ╰───────────────────────────╯
```

If you lost 50%, it will take a near miracle of 100% in gain to recoup the loss of 50%. This does not include fees paid along the way. Factoring in fees paid would only make this equation look more upsetting!

WHAT KEEPS YOU AWAKE AT NIGHT?

In case you are the rare person who doesn't mind paying unnecessary fees, in Chapter 4 we will illustrate how destructive fees can be to your portfolio.

"Compound interest is the eighth wonder of the world. He who understands it, earns it ... he who doesn't ... pays it." -  Albert Einstein

# Chapter Four

## Heather & Steve
## Hypothetical Example Case Study

Heather and Steve are siblings. Heather and her brother Steve both enjoyed amazing careers and were wise investors throughout their working years. In this example case study, we'll look at the overall effect of retiring in a stable financial environment versus an unstable environment. **Heather and Steve will each withdraw $40,000 Annually as supplemental retirement income.**

WHAT KEEPS YOU AWAKE AT NIGHT?

Heather enjoys her first four years of retirement. Heather's investments remain stable and she enjoys 4 consecutive years of growth.

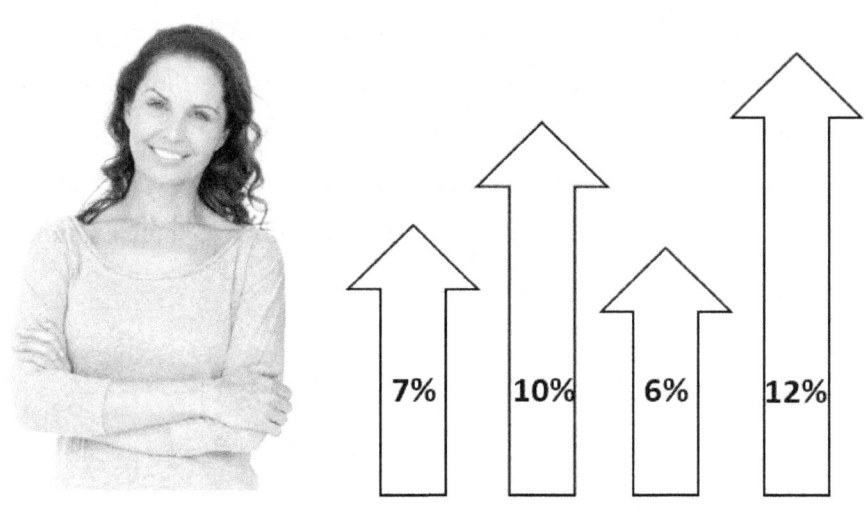

# YEAR 1

Heather's account earns 7%

bringing her account balance to $535,000.

Heather withdraws her $40,000 of retirement income bringing her adjusted account balance to $495,000.

# YEAR 2

Heather's account earns 10%
bringing her account balance to $544,500.

Heather withdraws her $40,000 of retirement income
bringing her adjusted account balance to $504,500.

# YEAR 3

Heather's account earns 6%
bringing her account balance to $534,770.

Heather withdraws her $40,000 of retirement income
bringing her adjusted account balance to $494,770.

# YEAR 4

Heather's account earns 12%
bringing her account balance to $554,142.

Heather withdraws her $40,000 of retirement income
bringing her adjusted account balance to $514,142.

WHAT KEEPS YOU AWAKE AT NIGHT?

Steve retires in an unstable environment and experiences 4 consecutive years of **the Rollercoaster Effect!**

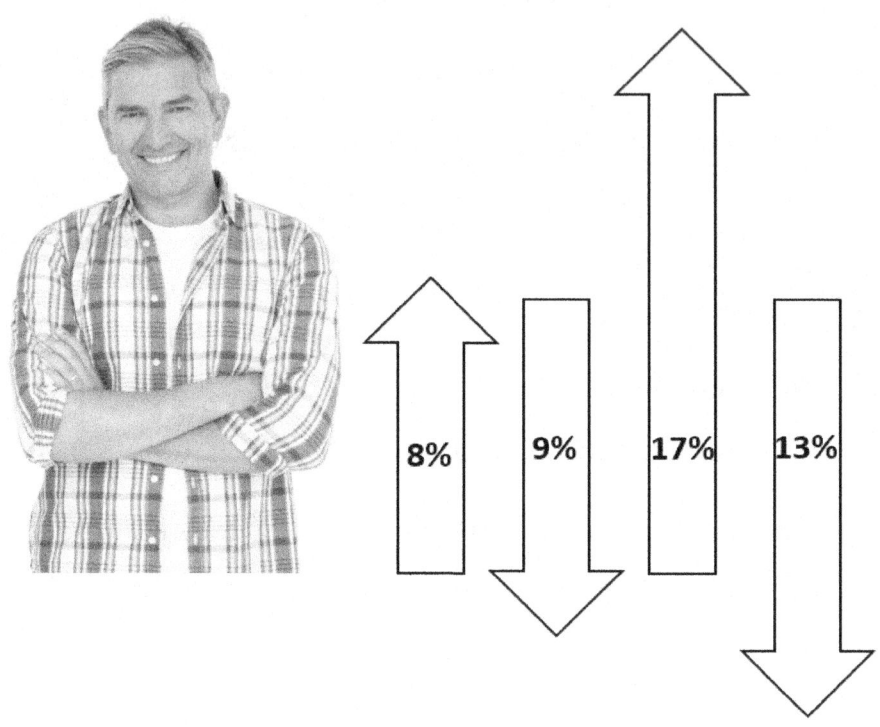

# YEAR 1

Steve's account earns 8%

bringing his account balance to $540,000.

Steve withdraws his $40,000 of retirement income

bringing his adjusted account balance to $500,000

WHAT KEEPS YOU AWAKE AT NIGHT?

# YEAR 2

Steve's account Loses 9%

bringing his account balance to $455,000.

Steve withdraws his $40,000 of retirement income
bringing his adjusted account balance to $415,000.

# YEAR 3

Steve's account earns 17%

bringing his account balance to $485,550.

Steve withdraws his $40,000 of retirement income
bringing his adjusted account balance to $445,550.

# YEAR 4

Steve's account Loses 13%

bringing his account balance to $387,629.

Steve withdraws his $40,000 of retirement income
bringing his adjusted account balance to $347,629.

**The Financial Scorecard shows that Steve has $166,513 Less in his retirement than his younger sister Heather.** Steve, being the older brother, retired four years before Heather. The problem wasn't anything more than bad timing. The moral to this tale is that nobody can predict the future and that bad timing can have devastating consequences.

## Fees, Fees and More Fees!

If you happen to work in the insurance arena or the world of financial services, this chapter will likely be the one that will cause you to close this book and walk away from it. For those of you reading this book that do not make your living in the Insurance or Financial Services Industry, allow me to explain the previous statement. **Fees!** Fees are a bit of a sensitive subject. As I've stated earlier in this book, I'm not against an insurance or financial professionals making a good living. I'm however, not a fan of unnecessary fees or hidden fees. The fact is that most policy owners and investors have no idea what they are paying in fees and what fees can do to the performance of their portfolio. My recommendation always, is to have a conversation with your agent or advisor and get some clarity on ALL the fees that you are paying. There are a great number of fees associated with The Insurance and Financial Services Industries. Fees seem to pop up like weeds but here are a few of the most common fees out there. **Management/Advisor Fees, Rider Fees,** Mortality and Expense Fees (M&E), Transaction Costs, **Wrap Fees,** Liquidation Fees, Hourly Fees, Etc., Etc., Etc.

## The Destructive Effect of a 1% Fee Over Time

Bob is a 60-year old man nearing retirement. He works for a wonderful company and has a career that he loves. Over his working years he has managed to save an additional $300,000. Bob's company offers a full pension and company stock to employees such as Bob. Shortly after his 60th birthday, Bob decides to invest his savings nest egg into some sort of investment plan. The following is a Hypothetical Example.

$300,000
Initial Investment

## Bob - Age 60

Bob stays invested from age 60 till age 85. His account does well and grows at a level 5% per year with no losses. He takes no distributions along the way. **Bob is paying a 1% Fee on his account annually.** Over the years he enjoys watching his account rise in value while being completely unaware of the effects of the 1% Fee that he has being paying.

WHAT KEEPS YOU AWAKE AT NIGHT?

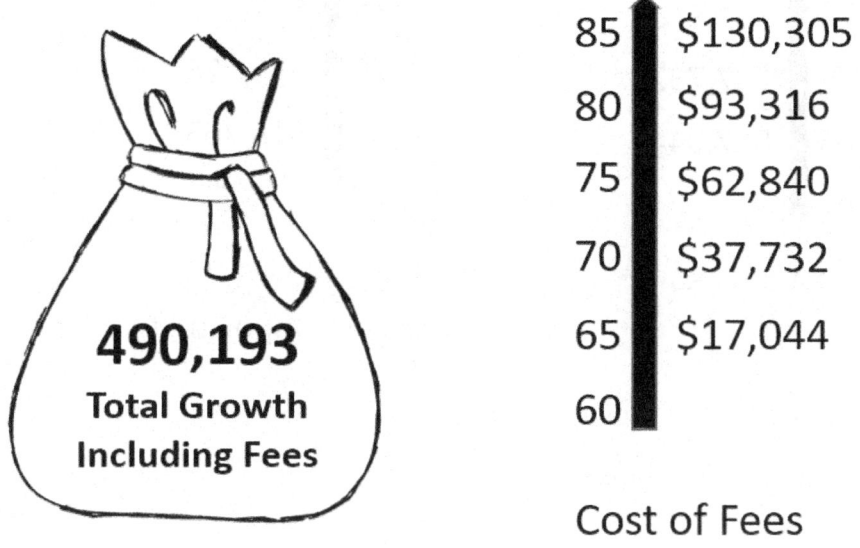

| | |
|---|---|
| 85 | $130,305 |
| 80 | $93,316 |
| 75 | $62,840 |
| 70 | $37,732 |
| 65 | $17,044 |
| 60 | |

**490,193**
Total Growth
Including Fees

Cost of Fees

Bob account grows by $490,193 bringing his overall account value to $790,193. Bob is paying $130,305 in fees over the twenty five-year period. But that is only part of the problem. It is always Important to factor in other effects such as Lost Opportunity Cost. Because Bob loses the opportunity to earn on the money lost to unnecessary fees, the effects of **Lost Opportunity Cost will cost him even more than the fee alone.**

WHAT KEEPS YOU AWAKE AT NIGHT?

| | | | |
|---|---|---|---|
| 85 | $130,305 | 85 | $225,713 |
| 80 | $93,316 | 80 | $144,944 |
| 75 | $62,840 | 75 | $87,279 |
| 70 | $37,732 | 70 | $46,725 |
| 65 | $17,044 | 65 | $18,765 |
| 60 | | 60 | |

Cost of Fees

Cost of Fees +
Lost Opportunity Cost

Over this twenty five-year period example, a simple 1% Fee could end up costing Bob over 225K between Fees Paid and the effects of Lost Opportunity Cost. **Bob's total account value without fees paid would have been $1,015,906.**

Source: fncalculator.com/mutualfundfeecalculator

WHAT KEEPS YOU AWAKE AT NIGHT?

# Chapter 5

## The Case For and Against Annuities  -  Part 1

## Types of Annuities

There are a number of different types of annuities and the differences are dramatic. At its core an annuity is a type of insurance product. Annuities are designed to provide income for people as they get older and begin to retire. Annuity Income Payments can be paid out monthly, quarterly, annually and in some cases in a lump sum. There are five basic types of annuity product categories out there. Variable, Fixed, Fixed-Indexed, Immediate or Deferred. Within those five categories there are many, many variations and options to consider. There are many different Fixed-Indexed Annuities for example, each with their own pros and cons. The same can be said about Variable Annuities. People tend to respond in one of three ways when the subject of annuities arises. Some people love them. Some people hate them. Some people have no idea how they work or what they really are. It is always important to get advice from someone that knows the advantages and disadvantages of all options. In this chapter we will look closer at the most common mistakes and misconceptions about annuities and why annuities are so misrepresented within the industry. We will also dive a bit deeper into what makes some annuities more *"ELITE"* than typical garden variety annuities and why most agents and advisors are completely unaware of such annuities.

WHAT KEEPS YOU AWAKE AT NIGHT?

## Common Misconceptions, Half Truths and Lies:

The general push back from the under informed, lower tier members of the financial services community are that annuities have high fees, hidden fees and/or high rider charges. Annuities have high surrender charges. Annuities are risky. Annuity withdrawal rates are low. Income Account Premium Bonuses are not real money. Annuities are often sold by insurance professionals whom earn commissions on the annuity sale. Unfortunately, this kind of misinformation leads some people to make decisions that are not always right for them. Many companies and advisors build their client marketing models around very lucrative fee-based, managed asset models. Some companies spend hours upon hours brainwashing… I meant, "training their financial services personnel" to create doubt about annuities. Once again, *kill it and redirect.* All of this is simply an effort to accumulate more assets to be managed and thus attempting to justify management fees charged as well as their very existence as "advisors."

Nothing is more terrible
than to see ignorance in action.
—Johann Wolfgang von Goethe

# THE TRUTH.

Most of what I just referenced pertains variable annuities or what we'll refer to as typical garden variety annuities. While all financial products may have their place in certain instances, a true professional will take the time to discuss options with you and help to make sure that your decision is right for you. **Fixed-Indexed Annuities** for example, can be a great solution for a person who is averse to market risk and wants to protect their hard-earned retirement account such as an IRA or a 401(k) while creating a stable income stream for their later years. Unlike other tax deferred accounts such as 401(k)'s and IRA's, Annuities have no contribution limit. However, not all annuities are created equally. FIA's can range from the standard garden variety type to what some would refer to as *"Elite"* for lack of a better word. If you know where to look you can sometimes discover what many others miss. There are FIA's out there that are void of unnecessary, excessive rider fees while still providing income for a lifetime in retirement without risk. In some cases, not just lifetime income but lifetime income that has the potential to increase over time even after the income rider has been initiated. **That is uncommon to say the least.** If the potential for increasing lifetime income wasn't enough, some of these unique annuity offerings also have very large initial premium/income account bonuses of 15% to 20% or more in some cases. There can also be annual index earnings crediting bonuses. These bonuses can add important increased financial value to a person's income withdrawals and in some cases add value to the estate in the case of the death of the account owner. Some accounts even offer increased income bonuses in times of poor health.

## When Earning 7% Guaranteed Equals 2.8% Net!

I had a recent experience with a client whom owned a variable annuity. I will admit upfront that I am Not a fan of variable annuities. The client was a referral of one of my established clients. In our first meeting we took an extensive look at their current accounts, policies and annuities and discussed an upcoming retirement date, needs, goals and plans. The one piece of their financial puzzle that seemed to be completely non-performing was their variable annuity. In getting to know my new client I asked how long they have had the annuity and what their original plan was for purchasing it. In the process this became an interesting case study. They told me that their previous advisor had set it up years ago and that it was a good one! *"A good one?"* I asked. Afterall, the account value was decreasing in recent years not increasing. What's more, I noticed a 1.3% fee on the account statement. My experience told me that the 1.3% fee was not the only thing dragging this account down. The client responded that they were told as a *"fact"* that the annuity account has a "guaranteed" 7% annual earning. I think most people would be happy if they earned 7% at least while only paying 1.3%. I asked my new client if I could see the rest of the account paperwork. Afterwards, we decided to make a call into the current insurance company and confirm a few details and find out why the account wasn't performing as well as the client had expected. The results were astonishing to the client, predictable to me. After getting a detailed breakdown from the insurance carrier as to management fees and rider charges we uncovered the total fee total for the variable account. The total fees were more like 4.2% NOT 1.3% as previously thought. Which makes a "guaranteed" 7% earn more like a 2.8%. What's more, this was a variable account which means it can increase in value *and* it can decrease in value based on economic factors. Those economic factors and the 4.2% in fees charged is why the account was losing money rather rapidly.

After careful analysis and thought, I was able to help my new client transfer over their variable annuity into a much better option considering their stage of life, growth and income needs. My client opted for an Elite Fixed Index Annuity and now benefits from growth without downside risk. Guaranteed Lifetime Income. No management fees and No rider fees plus some additional chronic health care coverage at No additional cost.

## A Brief Look at Annuity History

Annuities are truly one of the oldest and most established financial strategies in the world. Annuities can be traced back to Biblical Times. In Rome, Caesar gave annuities to roman soldiers returning from battle as financial rewards. Throughout history annuities have served as a vital part of the financial plan of millions of people including Beethoven, President Abraham Lincoln, Andrew Carnegie, Benjamin Franklin and Babe Ruth to name a few. Baseball Hall of Famer Babe Ruth survived the darkest days of the Great Depression and continued living in luxury until his death because his finances were protected against unnecessary market risk.

WHAT KEEPS YOU AWAKE AT NIGHT?

*"I may take risks in life,*
*but I will never risk my money, I use annuities and*
*I never have to worry about my money."*
*— Babe Ruth*

Ruth, like many others, found himself unemployed for the large part of the 1930's. The annuities that he had purchased between 1923 – 1929 during his baseball career is what kept the party going during one of the

WHAT KEEPS YOU AWAKE AT NIGHT?

darkest economic periods in US history. Ruth received a reported $17,500 per year from his annuities which equates to $290,000 in today's money.

If you are a sports fan you probably often hear about an athlete signing some sort of record deal. One hundred, two hundred or three hundred million-dollar sports contracts don't shock us as much as it did in years past. One of the biggest misunderstandings by the average sports fan is what these huge contracts consist of. Often the image people have is of yachts, champagne and taking long baths in tubs filled with cash! In reality, many of those long-term deals are annuity backed. Athletes can still get their hands on plenty of cash up front to buy big houses, expensive cars and take luxury vacations but often, the majority of the contract is paid out through annuity payments over a lifetime. Smart! And a true win/win for both the athlete and the team.

## The Bottom Line

There is no doubt that annuities have a strong history but while no single financial product, strategy or approach is right for everyone, annuities can often be the missing piece to a financial portfolio. The right annuity can provide a valuable hedge against unnecessary risk while creating lifetime income that can be counted on. Many, many millions of Americans rely on the principal of protecting and guaranteed lifetime income that annuities can provide.

WHAT KEEPS YOU AWAKE AT NIGHT?

# The Watercooler Effect

If there wasn't already enough confusion over complex financial matters allow me to add one more. It is called The Watercooler Effect or The Breakroom Effect. If you work for a company and take frequent trips to the breakroom, you'll likely run into *Mr. Know It All*. Every company has one. A person who gets a kick out of the idea that their opinion is important. Mr. Know It All, as I like to call this person, is often a man but not always. Mr. Know It All typically has just enough financial savvy and experience to be dangerous but not enough to be truly helpful. If you know the type of person that I'm referring to you'll also know that if you share your ideas, thoughts and concerns this person will usually tell you several ways to improve your life meanwhile their situation is often in a state of disarray.

WHAT KEEPS YOU AWAKE AT NIGHT?

You simply cannot allow an unqualified opinion to lead you down the wrong path. Seeking a Qualified Professional will always be your best move.

**66**
WHAT KEEPS YOU AWAKE AT NIGHT?

# Chapter Six

## The Case For and Against Annuities  -  Part 2

## The Battle Lines Have Been Drawn!

The annuity debate has turned into a feisty battle in recent years. Statistics show that billions upon billions upon billions of dollars have moved from typical, asset under management accounts (AUM) to annuities. Each year this number grows substantially as consumers become more educated and less influenced by financial product pushers and cookie cutter financial plans. As you might imagine, the dialogue has turned rather ugly, self-serving and predictively short sighted. So called "Online Research" can be a lot like wading into a cesspool. There has been an increase in *"Paid"* advertising online and on tv, radio and print. Usually paid ads are just carefully worded, general blanket statements that are merely opinions disguised as fact. Remember, the goal is to get you to call or request more information.

You may discover that the "Individual Plan and Advice" tailored to your "Specific Needs" is more generic that you had thought it was. Qualified Plans like 401(k)'s are often the worst in my humble opinion. People are all too often placed in allocations based upon age grouping and risk tolerances selections.

WHAT KEEPS YOU AWAKE AT NIGHT?

Helpful clues that might save you from becoming a financial statistic.

1.) Be cautious of carefully written "Blanket Statements" such as *"I Hate Annuities!"* Or *"Annuities Are Bad Investments!"* Or *"Annuities Are A Scam!"*

2.) Be cautious of variable annuity contracts if you are risk adverse.

3.) Get a detailed list of any and all fees charged as well as fund fee charges and surrender charges, etc., etc.

## Modern Portfolio Theory and Mr. Potato Head

The Modern Portfolio Theory came into existence in 1952 when economist Harry Markowitz wrote a dissertation on "Portfolio Selection." The Modern Portfolio Theory is alive today in the financial services industry. Markowitz believed that a diversified portfolio was less volatile and more stable for investors at that time. That all sounds good if you stop right there and don't ponder the obvious. All you need to do is to look around yourself a bit or turn on the television news for a moment or two. The world is a completely different place than it was in 1952. How many things that were viewed as "modern" in the 1950's would still be considered modern today? For starters, trades happen in seconds today as they took days to complete in 1952. We live in a plugged-in 24-hour news media environment. Global events that can shake up the financial world in mere minutes. Care to guess what was the #1 kid's toy in 1952? It was Mr. Potato Head. When was the last time you heard of Mr. Potato Head being perched at the top of a child's Christmas wish list?

The point of this is to get you, the reader to think. Shouldn't the financial industry step out of the 1950's and start adjusting to the 21$^{st}$ century now? If volatility wasn't an issue in the first place there would have been no place for the "Modern" Portfolio Theory. The last time I checked volatility was still causing financial havoc and devastation for many investors. The only difference is that now a devastating loss can cripple your retirement plan in the blink of an eye!

## Reconsidering an Old and Outdated 4% Rule

In 1994 Mr. William Bengen published a study based upon data that he had collected. The study ushered in the 4% Rule. Based upon his research, Mr. Bengen believed that retirees could take 4% of their initial investment as a distribution. This should make you wonder as to what percentage might be "the rule" if unnecessary fees and volatility wasn't an issue in the financial markets. More recently another more updated study was published by Wade Pfau a professor at the American College of Financial services. Professor Pfau gave clear notice that based upon his research, the 4% Rule should be replaced by the 3% Rule.

WHAT KEEPS YOU AWAKE AT NIGHT?

To make my point, below is a hypothetical example for illustration purposes only. This illustration depicts a $300,000 account value with annual distributions of 4%. This hypothetical illustration was based upon recent market history.

The light grey portion represents a market type of managed asset subject to risk exposure and management fees. The darker black portion represents an Elite type of Fixed Indexed Annuity (FIA). You can clearly see why so many American retirees are opting out of risky investments for the safety and security of a well-positioned FIA.

**Account Balance**

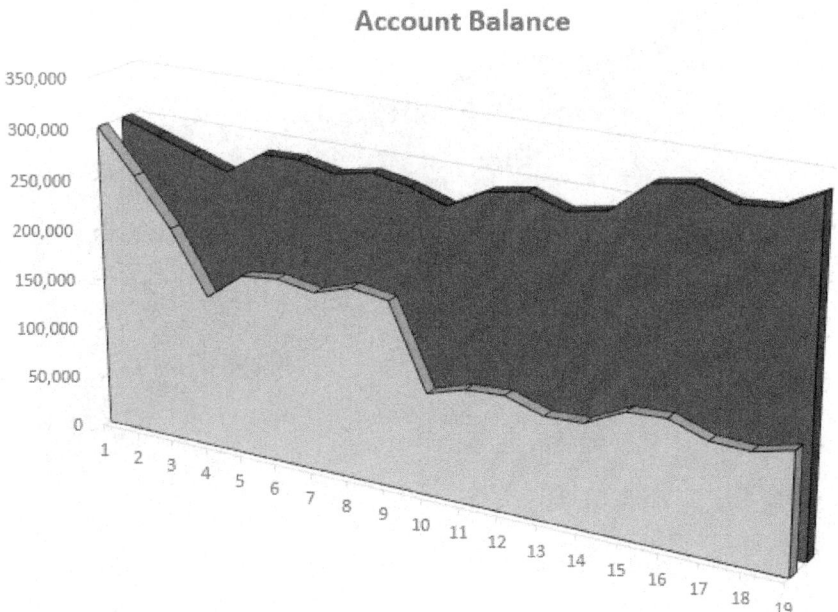

WHAT KEEPS YOU AWAKE AT NIGHT?

The illustration below the depicts a $300,000 account value with annual distributions of now 5%. This hypothetical illustration was based upon recent market history.

The light grey portion represents a market type of managed asset subject to risk exposure and management fees. The darker black portion represents an Elite type of Fixed Indexed Annuity (FIA).

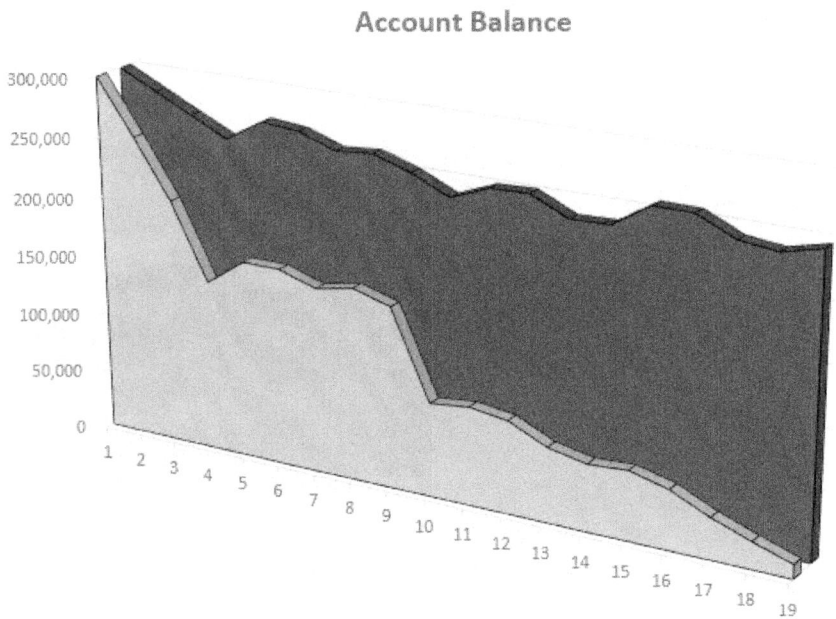

Account Balance

WHAT KEEPS YOU AWAKE AT NIGHT?

This third illustration below the depicts a $300,000 account value with annual distributions of now 6%. This hypothetical illustration was based upon recent market history.

The light grey portion represents a market type of managed asset subject to risk exposure and management fees. The darker black portion represents an Elite type of Fixed Indexed Annuity (FIA).

It's easy to see how a typical investment account can dwindle down to zero in a short amount of time while The FIA will payout income for life.

**Account Balance**

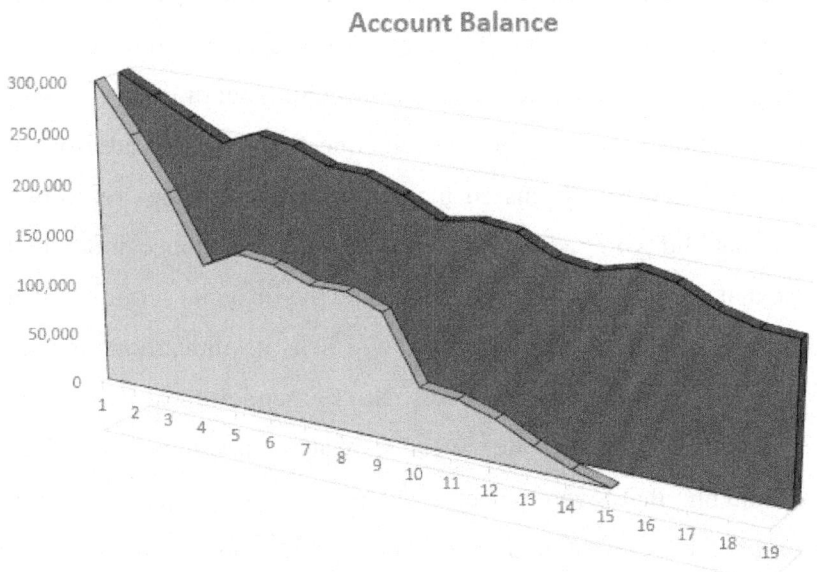

WHAT KEEPS YOU AWAKE AT NIGHT?

# A Man Named Felix

For a lot of retirees and people nearing retirement Income is King! I was introduced to a gentleman named Felix at a local event that I had attended recently. Felix was 6 months away from retiring and had lots of questions. What I found curious was the fact that Felix already had a financial advisor with a big firm who he had worked with for over a decade. Nevertheless, I thought I might be able to assist in answering a few of his questions without stepping on any toes. I found Felix sincere, intelligent and very worrisome. That isn't uncommon for someone 6 months out from closing out their career and beginning to see retirement on the horizon. What looked to be a quick conversation in the hallway turned into a 45 min discussion. The conversation seemed to hover around the topic of retirement income and a fear of running out of money. I asked Felix if he had discussed his thoughts and questions with his advisor. He said that yes, they had discussed these topics several times recently. I asked, "what did your advisor tell you Felix?" And once more in a response that never seems to go out of style in the financial services arena, his advisor wanted to keep him in a 100% accumulation account completely exposed to potential losses. Not to mention fees! Felix asked me if he could sit down with me to hear more about annuities. Particularly FIA's. I told him that I would meet with him under one condition. I asked Felix to go to his current advisor and ask him to construct a reasonable retirement income plan projection. I told him that once he had that in-hand to call me and we would meet up. I figured that there was a 50% chance at best that I would hear back from Felix once he revisited his current advisor. Afterall, human nature being what it is. To my surprise Felix called my office about five weeks or so later and scheduled a consultation. A few days ahead of our meeting Felix emailed me an income plan for lack of a better description that his advisor put together for him. The plan was littered with additional data on market averages and growth projections. In other words, this *"income plan"* was based upon nothing more than hope. Hope that the funds that Felix was invested in would not decline. Hope that a catastrophic financial event didn't take place during Felix's golden years.

Felix and I got down to the business of creating an Income Plan that he could actually count on. Felix told me at one point that he was so surprised at how much income a FIA could produce considering how determined his current advisor was to try to run FIA's down at every opportunity. I asked Felix to come up with a strong investment rate of return to compare against the Elite FIA that I was incorporating into our plan. Felix said 8%. He smiled and said "I know it's probably not a realistic figure" but he wanted to be optimistic. Felix was definitely an optimist if he thought 8% annually year after year was realistic without ever having a down year. But nonetheless, we proceeded with the analysis.

The final results were now in and Felix and I could discuss in detail the data that the income Planning software produced. Based upon the fact that Felix had right at $600,000 in his retirement account we compared his very optimistic perfect world investment account return of 8% vs the FIA. Even though the FIA's earning history was higher than what I calculated into

WHAT KEEPS YOU AWAKE AT NIGHT?

the comparison, I used a much lower number of 2.50% just to make the point. Felix's $600,000 in his managed/market-based account earning 8% would provide him with Immediate Retirement Income of $24,000 at a 4% withdrawal rate. Meanwhile, if the FIA earned only 2.50% it would produce $28,800 in Immediate Lifetime Retirement Income. Matter of fact, the managed market-based account would need to have a balance of $720,000 to simply match the FIA Income of $28,800. That's not all. **There are Three Additional Important Points to mention.**

1.) The Fixed Indexed Annuity will provide this income to Felix for Life without concerns about outliving his money.

2.) The managed market-based account projections of only $24,000 didn't account for annual fees paid and the possibility of loss.

3.) The FIA Income was calculated without the benefit of any Income Account Bonuses added. And Income Bonus would have added even more income than the $28,800.

To take this a step further let's Illustrate this scenario a different way. If Felix was in a position to defer the retirement income for 10 years, the numbers would show an even greater disparity. Using Felix's $600,000 in his managed/market-based account earning 8% would provide him with Deferred Retirement Income of $51,814. Meanwhile, if the FIA earned only 2.50% it would produce $58,177 in Deferred Lifetime Retirement Income. Finally, the managed market-based account would need to have a balance of $673,786 to simply match the FIA Income of $58,177.

WHAT KEEPS YOU AWAKE AT NIGHT?

So how is it that 2.50% can produce more in retirement income than an investment account earning 8%? Simply this, Annuities are created and constructed for income purposes first and foremost. Unlike an investment account and the standard 3-4% distribution parameters, Annuities are built to allow for higher percentages of income payouts than other investments. Additionally, some annuities offer premium bonuses in the double-digit range. These premium bonuses help to drive up the income account values.

**Higher Income Payout Percentages + Higher Income Account Values = Higher Income Payouts.**

It is also important to note that Lifetime Annuity Income Payouts can be received as single life income or joint life income. Variable annuities are unpredictable and often have high fees. However Fixed Indexed Annuities (FIA) provide the advantages listed above without additional unnecessary fees or exposure to risk. In the case of a couple with an FIA for instance with a single life annuity income account, the income is paid till the death of the policy owner. In the case of joint life income, the payout continues till the death of both individuals. You cannot outlive your money. The lifetime income election pays out income even if you live to some advanced age and the base account is out of funds. The income continues until death. Conversely, managed investment accounts cannot make that promise.

77

**78**

WHAT KEEPS YOU AWAKE AT NIGHT?

# Chapter Seven

## Change Your Thinking, Change Your Outcome. The Choice Is Yours!

There is a thin line that separates successful people from unsuccessful people. The line is so thin it's hard for most to see but it's there. *So why do some people seem to possess this slight edge over people?* Let me give you my prospective as a person who has worked with and consulted many people over a long period of time. I find that there are typically two very predominant personality types. One type wants to learn as much as they can about a subject like finances. This person will seek information and ask a lot of questions throughout that process. Ultimately, this person usually makes good decisions. The other personality type typically wants to know only what they need to know to get by. This person is the type of person that makes the larger financial services industry really click. I know that might seem harsh but it's true. The second personality type that I referenced usually gives up quickly when it comes to learning about a topic such as finances and simply throws up their hands and march into the nearest financial company's office and say, *"you take this!"* Unfortunately, this isn't likely to ever change. But if that person is you, not to worry, there will always be a smiling face in a suit ready to take your money and place it somewhere...**for a fee, that is!**

WHAT KEEPS YOU AWAKE AT NIGHT?

# Separating Fact from Fiction

Are you the type of person who truly wants to make good decisions? Decisions that you won't have to live with in regret later-on. then you'll need to start by separating fact from fiction. The chapters leading up to this point I tried to challenge you to look and see beyond the hype and marketing noise. Remember these key points. Avoid anyone who make untethered blanket statements such as "I Hate Annuities!" Or "Insurance is a Bad Investment!" Or "Wall Street Has Historically Out-performed Everything Out There!" Or "You Have To Risk Big To Win Big!" These sort of statements and claims come from a wide range of financial advisors and insurance agents. In just about all cases, the person stating that they dislike or even hate any product or strategy simply has another product that they want to try to sell you. If this approach didn't work, you would never hear these sorts of low level, half sighted opinions. The problem is that they work all too well on *"some people."*

While annuities can add significant value, protection, income and peace of mind, there are other necessary elements when creating a retirement plan or estate plan such as wills and trusts, life insurance and legacy. Whole Life Insurance is a mainstay in most estate plans. The right kind of life insurance can provide protection and growth while doing so in a taxed advantaged environment. Sadly however, many people have heard the loud barking of the anti-life insurance crowd. By the way, that crowd isn't as big and loud as it used to be. Nonetheless there is still some idol yapping!

WHAT KEEPS YOU AWAKE AT NIGHT?

Back in Chapter Three I illustrated "The Dark Side Of Compound Interest." One of the biggest mistakes average investors make is living in the moment. I recall a large market crash some years ago. You might as well recall one too. The crash was large enough that it took a number of years to gain back what was lost in that particular crash. Seven and even eight years later people were finally rejoicing about the fact that they had recovered their losses from that crash years ago. I recall having this debate with a young financial advisor. In his defense he was still in school when this crash took place. Therefore, he entered the industry during the rebound years and lacked a balanced perspective. He argued with youthful glee that yes, the markets may have tanked some time ago but if a person stayed invested *(And Continued to Pay Management Fees I suppose),* such a person would have eventually made it all back. My response was to ask this question, *"what about the lost years?"* All he managed to give me in response to the question was a puzzled look. Being inquisitive minded, I had to ask another question hoping for some sort of intelligible response. I asked him, *"What about the investor's average rate of return?"* Again, silence fell over the young man. Assuming the conversation had gone as far as it could I wished him a good day and began to head out to an upcoming appointment with a client. The young financial advisor dashed up to me and said the following, "My clients averaged over 17% last year!" Wow! I said. *What about the Average Rate of Return over the period of years that the account values were climbing up out of the hole that the previous crash took them into*? Again, no answer. Had I not been in a hurry to get to my meeting, I would have happily helped to educate him on the subject. I am always willing to try to help where I can.

WHAT KEEPS YOU AWAKE AT NIGHT?

# The Late Great Average Rate of Return Myth

In this section I will use a very simplistic, hypothetical example to show how an average rate of return can be a bit misleading and one dimensional and once and for all bury the myths that cloud the subject. This example doesn't take in consideration things such as management fees paid and overall investment objectives. This is just a basic exercise in understanding positive or negative effects of a rate of return spread out over a period of four years.

For this example, using any investment that you may have in mind. let's use a return of 10% in year one. A lot of people would take a 10% return and be very happy. Using this example, if you had started your investment with $100,000 and you gained 10%, your investment would have earned $10,000 bringing your account value to around $110,000. I say to around $110,000 because that doesn't account for expenses or fees charged which would lower the amount of growth. Still not a bad year overall. But we've all heard the old expression, what goes up, must come down.

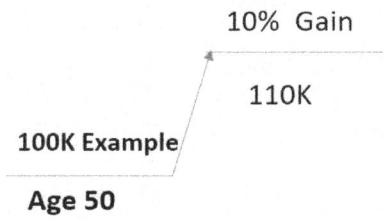

10% Gain

110K

100K Example

Age 50

For example, lets now illustrate a much greater earning over several years. Hypothetically speaking, if a 50-year old man, let's call him Mark, began investing with that same $100,000 and was willing to live with both good years and bad years. The investment will likely level out some over a period of time. I realize that not all people are optimistically minded. However, people whom experienced painful financial losses in the recent past are likely to be a bit more pessimistic instead. In this hypothetical example, Mark invests his $100,000 and doesn't get a mere 10% return. No, Mark actually earned 100%. Mark is now on cloud nine and feeling just fine about his investment decision. His $100,000 has increased to a whopping $200,000 in just one year.

WHAT KEEPS YOU AWAKE AT NIGHT?

In the second year the investment declined by 50%. Mark is now faced with the unfortunate fact that his account has a value around where he began with at $100,000. Again, I say to around $100,000 because that doesn't account for expenses or fees charged which would lower the amount of growth. But Mark is an optimist and decides to roll the dice and stay invested.

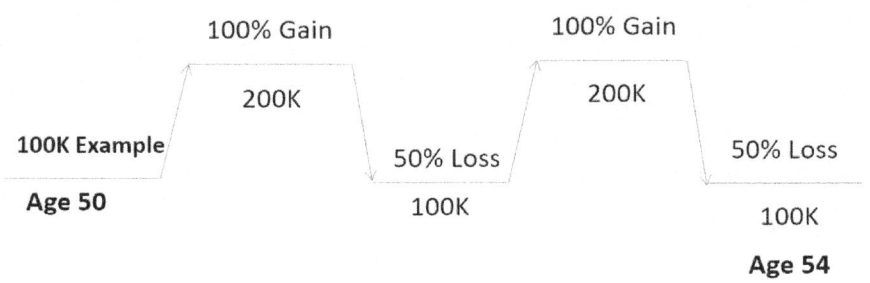

In the third year the investment increases by 100%. Mark's account value is back up to $200,000 once again. The stars appear to have realigned and Mark is back on top. All seems right again in his world again. But to be fair, let's not forget that old saying, *"what goes up, must come down."*

In the fourth year of this example, the investment decreases by 50% of its value once again. Mark, now 54 years old sees his account value is back to where it was four years ago when he was only 50. ***Ouch!*** But that's not the worst part of this example. Mark's average rate of return over the 4-year period is actually a whopping 25%. ***What???***

WHAT KEEPS YOU AWAKE AT NIGHT?

In case you are thinking that this illustration involves some sort of voodoo figures or that this doesn't add up, grab your calculator and let's break it down. First, let's add up the increases in years 1 and 3. Then let's add up the decreases in years 2 and 4.

1st Year 100%  +  3rd Year 100%  =  200% in collective increases.

2nd Year 50%  +  4th Year 50%  =  100% in collective decreases.

Next subtract the collective decreases from the collective increases.

200% collective increases, minus 100% collective decreases = 100%

Next divide the four-year collective increase by the 4 years invested.

100% Divided by 4 (years) = **25% Average Rate of Return.**

In this hypothetical example we illustrated, decreases are only half of the overall percentage of the overall increases. Mark would probably tell you that his return more feels like a zero not 25% on average. The problem is timing. If casino gamblers would simply gather up and cash in their chips after a win a lot of casinos would be out of business. Human nature is what keeps casinos open and people continuing to risk it all. Human nature is also what Wall Street feasts on. The difference is that millions of

**85**

WHAT KEEPS YOU AWAKE AT NIGHT?

Americans gamble every day in the markets by simply betting their retirements and financial health on something that they have little to no control over.

In chapters five and six we dove into The Case For and Against Annuities. Elite FIA's to be exact. There is no denying the fact that the right annuity can be a great piece of your financial game-plan as FIA's can offer Preservation of your hard-earned money better than anything I've seen in my career. **Not only can FIA's protect money, but they can earn solid competitive rates of return (Accumulation) without the risk of downside loss.**

WHAT KEEPS YOU AWAKE AT NIGHT?

The main issue with annuities if there is one, is access to large sums of cash for purchases, acquisitions or investments. This is also a point that the anti-annuity advisors like to state whenever possible. A defense mechanism taught to them by their employers. Chapter Eight will be dedicated to an Accumulation Strategy that might blow your mind. But again, it is also one of the most misunderstood and misrepresented concepts in the financial services and insurance industries. **The Banking Policy Strategy™ provides Safety, Accumulation, Leverage, Control and Legacy.**

*"The study of money, above all other fields in economics, is one in which complexity is used to disguise truth or to evade truth, not to reveal it."*

## - John Kenneth Galbraith
## Professor of Economics Harvard University

## 88
WHAT KEEPS YOU AWAKE AT NIGHT?

# Chapter Eight

## The Banking Policy Strategy®

The Banking Policy Strategy® has been around for a longtime and has been used by Banks, Corporations, People of Great Wealth and many average everyday Americans as a **Dynamic Wealth Building, Personal System of Finance.** Over the years the strategy has been referred in various titles such as The Banking Policy Strategy®. Most notably, The Infinite Banking Concept® (IBC) which was coined by R. Nelson Nash of The Infinite Banking Institute. Speaking personally, my wife and I have utilized the strategy in our own personal scenario for well over a decade. Below are just a few of the main benefits.

1.) **Leverage!**
2.) **Non-Direct Recognition**
3.) **A Personal System of Finance**
4.) **Tax Advantaged Life Insurance**
5.) **Contractual Agreement/Stability**
6.) **Wealth Creation Limited by Your Own Imagination!**
7.) **Estate and Legacy Planning**

WHAT KEEPS YOU AWAKE AT NIGHT?

# The Topic of Insurance

Like most good things in life, timing isn't always what we would have preferred it to be. What I mean is that I have heard countless people, including myself, utter the words "I wish I had heard about this 20-years earlier." The reason you've probably have not heard of The Banking Policy Strategy or The Infinite Banking Concept® is because of how the topic of insurance is too often represented. For centuries, insurance has been widely thought of as a benefit that your family receives after you die. In other words, you must die in order to get the benefit out of it. That's not a popular selling feature. It may be a needed benefit but far from a popular one. In the 1970's a man named A.L. Williams pushed forth his belief centered around "Buy Term and Invest the Difference" and he became very wealthy in the process. Thankfully the BTID strategy has fallen out of favor and is widely considered to be just an unfortunate chapter in the history of the insurance industry. Only a few self-prescribed radio and television financial personalities still try to sell that old snake oil recipe.

Along comes the Banking Policy Strategy, AKA the Infinite Banking Concept. This isn't a new approach but an old one. As you might imagine, various books have been written on the subject. Immediately insurance agents whom had started to grow weary of trying to make a career out of selling death benefit now had a new and improved way to market insurance policies. I remember one insurance agent approaching me at a

Banking Policy Strategy conference that I was speaking at and said that *"Infinite Banking saved his career."* In ten short minutes it was apparent to me that this career insurance agent had No idea what the concept was about. Not to mention, the policies he was selling as "Banking Policies" were not what would be considered the correct type of insurance.

Over the last decade plus, I have trained and developed hundreds of insurance and financial professionals on the proper design of the Banking Concept. The one thing that still baffles me from time to time is how many agents struggle to explain a simple strategy or concept. I can't even count the number of experienced agents and advisors I've watched fall face down trying to explain the strategy based on analysis.

**Remember as we dive deeper into this strategy, it is 80% Concept and 20% Numbers. In other words, 80% Concept & 20% Insurance.**

WHAT KEEPS YOU AWAKE AT NIGHT?

# The Formula = Success!

A properly Designed Whole Life Policy built for "Banking" is Uniquely different policy than the traditional whole life policy that you may be familiar with. The formula is simple, but it is hard to find all the necessary pieces.

## The Right Advisor + The Right Insurance Company – Unnecessary Insurance Expenses + The Right Insurance Policy + A Flexible PUA Rider + Term Rider – MEC Issues ÷ Strategic Plan of Action = Success!

WHAT KEEPS YOU AWAKE AT NIGHT?

If you have the right formula, you can Build Wealth that is only limited by your own imagination. Let's start by highlighting the Key Benefits.

# Benefits of Infinite Banking

1. ## Safe, Secure Wealth:
   - Eliminate market exposure & risk.
   - Recapture wealth that is currently being transferred away.
   - Contractual Growth – Tax Benefits
   - Protection from creditors, judgments and law suits.

2. ## Non Direct Recognition:
   - Liquidity – quick access to money w/o restrictions.
   - Outstanding loans do not inhibit growth.

# Benefits of Infinite Banking

3. ## Tax Free Retirement Plan:
   - Reliable, predictable retirement income.
   - Money can be withdrawn **Tax Free!**
   - Continued Growth even if you become disabled.
   - Built-in Chronic Care Benefits.

4. ## Legacy:
   - Financial Security for your loved ones.
   - A strategy that can be passed on to future generations.

WHAT KEEPS YOU AWAKE AT NIGHT?

# Leverage, Leverage, Leverage!

It is often said in the real estate industry that the three most important words in RE are *location, location, location*. In the world of Banking the three most important words are *Leverage, Leverage, Leverage*. Chartered Banks know a thing or two about turning a profit. I'm not simply referring to fees. Although most people are familiar with paying many various fees that banks often charge, banks earn insane rates of return. **How insane?** Imagine High Double Digits or even Triple Digit Earnings! *How do banks make those sorts of earnings? LEVERAGE!*

**A Quick, Simplistic, Hypothetical Example of Leverage in 6 Steps.**

1.) Leo deposits $100,000 in his bank account with his local branch.

2.) Leo earns 3% Simple Interest on his money.

3.) Over the course of 1 year, Leo receives $3,000 in interest earned.

4.) Because of Fractional Banking and the backing of the FDIC, Leo's bank lends the $100,000 to a small business for 90 days at 12% Interest. 12% Interest on $100,000 over 3 Months = $3,000. The bank could charge 2% in loan fees to the business = $2,000. In this hypothetical example, the bank earns $5,000 in 90 days.

5.) Leo's bank could duplicate that cycle 4 times in one year. That would add up to $20,000 in one year, **Using Leo's Money!**

6.) Divide the banks investment of $3,000 (Leo's Interest of 3%) by the $20,000 that the bank earned by lending out Leo's money = 667% rate of return on the bank's original investment of $3,000.

WHAT KEEPS YOU AWAKE AT NIGHT?

**Leverage is King**. While average Joe out there is simply seeking a solid rate of return on their money…Banks, Corporations and Wealthy Individuals seek leverage. Financially speaking, with the right leverage in your hand, you could move mountains!

# Non-Direct Recognition

**This is a Big One!** Pay close attention. This gets missed by most consumers, insurance agents and financial advisors. Without this key piece, you might as well kiss the advantage of gaining financial leverage goodbye. Non-Direct Recognition, put simply, means that policy loans do not affect policy dividend earnings. During my years in the field I have only come across a small handful of Dividend Paying Whole Life Insurance Companies that have the type of policies that are needed for The Banking Policy Strategy.

In my attempt to save any confusion, let me say it this way. Borrowing money from an insurance policy isn't unique. Paying simple loan interest on the money you borrow from the insurance company's general fund is completely common. Policy loan interest typically ranges from the 4-5% range. What Non-Direct Recognition provides is a way to take a policy loan and benefit from leverage. Many insurance companies report annual dividend earnings at 5.5% - 7.5% or possibly higher on some occasions.

It is Important to note, these Banking Policy Concepts do NOT rely solely on simply earning a dividend. Dividends in a standard investment vehicle are everything. They serve as a measuring rod as to how the investment is doing. **Dividends earned in a properly designed banking policy are merely the frosting on top of the dessert.** "Banking" is what you do with the tools. You can refer to the hypothetical example at the beginning of this chapter as a refresher. It is also just as important to note that a policy owner doesn't necessarily need to take money out to build high earnings if a policy is properly designed.

## A Personal System of Finance

Creation of your Personal System of Finance comes down to properly educating yourself on any advantages or disadvantages within your personal scenario. **I would highly recommend that you seek council from a Certified Banking Policy Advisor versus the typical insurance agent, financial advisor or an internet search.** Finding the best person to help you build a plan and properly design the policy will be well worth while. You'll sometimes hear this system of finance described as a family banking system. In the business world it's often referred to as a corporate financing tool. Whatever you choose to call it is up to you. The bottom line is that the right design could provide a vehicle to grow and leverage wealth beyond most things you may have previously heard of.

# Tax Advantaged Life Insurance

Let's be clear on two things. First, this information is Not intended to be taken as tax advice. You would require a CPA for that advice. Second, The Banking Policy Strategy is Not a method of dodging taxes. Insurance policies simply have built-in tax advantages that other financial products do not. Policy loans for example are not considered taxable because they are a loan, not a liquidation or distribution like you might see in the investment arena. Death benefits are typically viewed as non-taxable events. This is largely why insurance policies are so heavily utilized in the estate planning field especially in the area of trusts. State tax laws can vary greatly from state to state. It is always advised that you ask an expert regarding what if any tax ramifications may exist in your specific state.

# Contractual Agreement/Stability

What attracts so many Banks, Corporations and wealthy people to life insurance are the strength and stability of the insurance companies themselves. There is a reason that Life Policies and Annuities are in high demand today. When you look at the skyline in most major metropolitan cities you typically see the names of banks and insurance companies at the tops of the tallest buildings. **That didn't just happen accidently!**

WHAT KEEPS YOU AWAKE AT NIGHT?

Throughout U.S. history, insurance companies are often the one's helping to get other industries and businesses back up and functioning financially after financial crisis. In most cases, when you are dealing with an insurance company you are dealing with a very stable 100 plus year-old established company with a strong dividend paying history.

In the case of traditional whole life contracts, the policy endows or matures at a certain age sometimes age 100. Sometimes age 120 or 121. What you will typically see when you look at the final year of a policy illustration is the cash value being equal to the death benefit. Which means, if should you live till the policy endows, you'll get the cash value because the death benefit is no more. What is important to understand is the fact that the policy works off a Contractual Algorithmic Calculation. Why is this piece so Important to understand? **Policy Banking!**

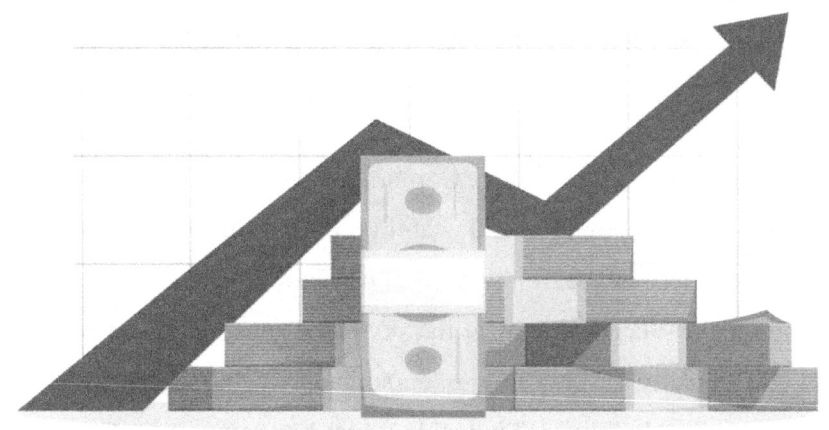

WHAT KEEPS YOU AWAKE AT NIGHT?

The more you utilize the properly designed policy for banking needs, such as debit reduction or asset accumulation, the bigger the policy gets. The bigger the policy gets, the higher the policy dividend earnings are. Remember **the Power of The Contract**. Proper utilization of the policy to build wealth contractually obligates the insurance company to pay you higher dividends in order to keep the **Contractual Algorithmic Calculation** on track for endowment.

## Wealth Creation Limited Only By Your Imagination!

Imagine for a moment that you were able to recapture dollars that you were throwing away every day to banks and financial companies. *Would that potentially be a lot of money?* You bet it would! It has been estimated that most Americans will buy and finance more in purchases and expenses than they will ever earn in their investments and savings accounts. *Don't believe it?* Banks and Financial Firms Do. Matter of fact, they are "Banking" on that very thing! **The Banking Policy Strategy allows an individual policy owner to mimic what a large bank does to leverage money and make returns in the process.** The strategy provides a means to do so in a safe, contractual environment. The amount of banking that a person can do is limited to the size of the policy owned. The larger the policy, the more opportunity you'll create for yourself. In traditional death benefit insurance scenarios, individuals are always looking for the greatest death benefit for the least amount of premium. In banking policy scenarios, individuals look for the *least* amount of death benefit coverage. IE, Insurance costs. In this scenario policy owners are looking to get as much into the policies as they can afford without triggering a Modified Endowment Contract.

The Modified Endowment Contract (MEC) was passed into law by congress in 1988. The MEC Law is simply put, a tax qualification for life insurance. If cumulative premiums exceed Federal Tax Law Limits a policy is deemed to have failed the 7-Pay Test and becomes a MEC. A MEC mean the policy becomes taxable and once a MEC, always a MEC.

**THIS IS EXACTLY WHY YOU NEED TO SPEAK TO AN EXPERT** and not simply a typical insurance agent or financial advisor. **Construction is Critical.** Properly Constructed, The Banking Policy Strategy could be the better than anything you've likely experienced. Remember, **it's about the Banking!**

Important to remember, if an insurance agent or financial advisor designs a policy based on direct recognition, you do Not have a banking policy. If you have a Universal Life Policy, you do Not have a banking policy. If you cannot contribute more than dividends to the paid-up addition rider, you do Not have a banking policy.

Incorrectly Constructed, The Banking Policy Strategy is no better than any other random insurance or investment product out there.

WHAT KEEPS YOU AWAKE AT NIGHT?

# Estate and Legacy Planning

Recently I was put in contact with a couple in their early 80's who were excited about The Banking Policy Strategy. The couple had a significant estate and wanted to make sure that their grandchildren inherited the majority of what they had amassed over their lifetimes. I brought in an established estate attorney to co-council them on the advantages of a trust versus a will. Once those particular questions had been addressed, I got to work on designing a Banking Policy Strategy for them. Being the fact that both the husband and wife were at an age that precluded them from being insured we ultimately opted to insure one of their adult children now age 50. The policy was structured like any other properly designed banking policy. My new senior clients now had a fully functional banking policy based upon the insured life of their daughter. The beneficiaries were the 2 grandchildren at 50% each.

The policy was created so that upon death of the senior co-owners of the policy, the contingent owner, their daughter becomes the new owner. Meanwhile the grandchildren are still the policy beneficiaries at 50% each. Sometime down the road when the mother passes on, the children inherit the estate that started with their Grand Parents in a tax advantaged position. That is merely one of many examples of a 3 Generation Estate.

## "You finance everything you buy…You either pay interest to someone else, or you give up interest you could have earned somewhere else. There are no exceptions."

### -Nelson Nash
### *The Infinite Banking Concept*®

If you are like most of my clients, you would probably want your estate to go to whom you please and not to end up in probate or worse. Building a proper Estate Plan is a wise thing to consider unless you think that you will live forever. My recommendation would be to visit The National Institute of Certified Estate Planners® (NICEP). You can find a Certified Estate Planner at NICEP.org.

# Chapter Nine

## Building an Income Plan

Whenever I am meeting with a client who is retired or approaching a retirement date, I generally like to start the conversation with a discussion about retirement income needs and cash availability concerns. All clients are different, and clients have distinctively different goals and concerns. However, the one common thread that all seem to share is the desire to protect what they have. **Here are the most frequently asked questions from new clients during our initial meeting.**

1.) Do I have enough money accumulated to retire?  OR
   Am I at risk of outliving my finances?
2.) How can I protect my finances from risk?
3.) What should I do for quick cash access should an unexpected need arise?
4.) What happens to my estate when I die?

There are other questions that are usually mentioned but these are far and away the most common concerns. Once more, as you can see by this

WHAT KEEPS YOU AWAKE AT NIGHT?

point of the book, that I am not a person who believes in unnecessary risk or fees. I believe very much in diversification. To address the most commonly asked questions I recommend starting with creating an inventory of assets and income streams both current and future such as social security income or pension payments. Equally as important is gathering a budget of known expenses and potential future financial needs. With this data we can begin to construct the beginnings of an Income Plan. It is not a difficult exercise but an essential first step. Once the outline of the plan is on paper it is easy to see if a person is in a good income position or if there is an income gap for instance. Often, I see that when there is a gap, additional distributions have been taken out along the way to fill the income need. That is not necessarily good or bad it just depends on the individual and the resources that they have. Numbers are black & white and remain unemotional. The numbers always tell us where we need to go with the income plan.

**The success of any income plan hinges on predictability of income.** I have seen plans from advisors and companies which I will not name that leave much to chance. I remember a lady named Margaret whom I met with a couple of years ago. I was in the middle of designing an income plan for her when she produced an income plan that her previous advisor built for her. I looked it over more to satisfy my own curiosity more than anything else. It was easy to see why her income plan wasn't holding up now that she was 5 years into her retirement. Why was the plan failing? The income projections were based on a portfolio that was still very much

WHAT KEEPS YOU AWAKE AT NIGHT?

exposed to market volatility and higher than average fees. The plan centered on a 4% distribution rate on her managed investment accounts. Recent years had taken a significant bite out of those accounts and 4% distribution wasn't providing the income that she needed. Margaret told me that at one point her old advisor mentioned something about "the safe money" versus "the growth money." Her advisor had put some of her money in fixed indexed annuities (FIA's) to create safety and guaranteed income but not enough was allocated there as it turns out. The "Growth Money" or "Invested Money" was in freefall. Important to note, the portion of her portfolio that was described as the growth or invested money should also be labeled the "Unsafe Money." If Margaret's Safe Money (FIA) account had been large enough to supply all the necessary income that she needed in retirement I would have had far less issue with it. Afterall, if she had the income required for her lifestyle, I guess she could gamble the rest if she wished. The bottom-line flaw was the portfolio allocation. Margaret could have had all her investments in a safe position both the monies allocated for income as well as the monies allocated for growth.

## Hope is Not a Strategy!

Predictability of income should not be left to chance. Too many people end up relying on hope versus predictability. **While it's nice to have hope, it is far better to have peace of mind!**

WHAT KEEPS YOU AWAKE AT NIGHT?

# The Amazing Superhero Named Zero!

Ask just about anyone who has ever suffered great losses within their financial portfolios if they would have been happy with a Zero instead of a loss. Although a zero doesn't sound exciting, a zero can save your

WHAT KEEPS YOU AWAKE AT NIGHT?

retirement. Imagine for a moment, every time the markets were doing well you made a competitive rate of return. Meanwhile, your account values were completely protected against loss in the bad years. **That's the Power of Zero!** I received a referral of a potential new client very recently. Like most of my referrals, an existing client told his golf buddy Jordan to give me a call. Jordan called my office and set up a consultation meeting. Jordan's case was an interesting one as Jordan was in the midst of his 20th year with his current financial advisor. With the first 19 years already in the books Jordan was happy with his advisor, happy with his portfolio performance and optimistic about the future. After hearing this I inquired as to what made him set the appointment. As it turned out, Jordan had an old 401(k) he was considering moving or rolling over and he had been reading up on fixed indexed annuities as of late. His advisor wanted to simply move that account into a managed account with his firm.

Over the course of a couple of weeks I was able to help Jordan by rolling over his 401(k) to an elite type of FIA. Thus, protecting that account against unnecessary risk and fees while securing lifetime income for retirement.

But is only half of the story. Jordan was very happy that I was easily able to help with his 401(k) rollover. He had grown very comfortable with me and my staff during those weeks. Sometime after, Jordan paid me another visit. This time he had a question that had been **keeping him awake at night.** He asked me to help analyze how an FIA would have performed over the last 19 years versus his current account.

This time Jordan has account statements in his hand and questions on his mind. Using financial software, I was able to clearly show him the

**107**

difference in the two scenarios side-by-side. We started by comparing his managed account earnings in the first year to the historical earnings of the FIA that he really liked. Over that period of 19 years, Jordan's managed account which began at $500,000 would have grown to $852,972 with a few more good years than bad years. However, once we subtracted the management fee of 1% the account balance was only $706,159. What really jumped off the page was what I showed him next. I illustrated his published earnings in his managed account including his 1% to the same account earning with two adjustments. First, I removed the six negative years in the 19-year account history and replaced those losses with Zero. Secondly, I cut the positive year earnings in half. So, in a year when he may have earned say, 12.78% I reduced the earning from that figure down to a mere 6.39%. Again, just to be clear, we replaced his losses with 0.00% and cut his earnings by 50%. The results were an eye opener for Jordan. By the end of the 19th year his account, even with a 1% fee would have grown to $961,264 instead of the $706,159 that he currently had. This exercise clearly showed that financial savviness isn't about chasing a fleeting rate of return number. *Truly savvy investors understand that simply eliminating losses will likely put you ahead in the long run versus risking everything to chase after an earning rate.*

Through this analysis, Jordan came to realize that while his account didn't do poorly and his advisor was a nice guy, he could have done much better. On that day, Jordan met **The Amazing Superhero Named Zero!**

WHAT KEEPS YOU AWAKE AT NIGHT?

# Creating a Blended Strategy

Creating a Blended Strategy is the best approach for most people. A blended strategy secures needed income that a person can count on for a lifetime while also creating the necessary cash reserves for additional needs or unexpected economic concerns or simply more leisure time at some exotic Caribbean resort. In the more recent chapters of this book we've delved into Fixed Indexed Annuities (FIA's) and The Banking Policy Strategy® in some detail. Both approaches have contractual guarantees in place that make them far more desirable to most people. Both approaches are designed to fill a specific need. My clients are always quick to point out that knowing that all of their hard-earned assets are insulated from unnecessary market risk and management fees, they now sleep better a night.

As always, my advice is to seek out the best help and advice that you can find. Do your research. Ask a lot of questions. A Fixed Indexed Annuity and/or a Banking Policy Blended Strategy may or may not be right for you. But it also may be exactly what you've been searching for.

**The following may help you determine if an FIA/Banking Policy Blended Strategy is something that you should consider. If you are looking for:**

1.) Safe, Secure Accumulation
2.) No risk of principal loss
3.) No Unnecessary or Hidden Fees
4.) Guaranteed Lifetime Income
5.) Access to Cash when needed without diminishing earnings (NDR)
6.) Ability to turn liabilities into assets like a banker would
7.) Built-In Additional Critical Care Protection
8.) Wealth Limited by Your Own Imagination!
9.) Tax Advantaged Retirement
10.) Tax Advantaged Estate/Legacy

**It might be worth your time to look into a FIA/Banking Policy Blended Strategy!**

WHAT KEEPS YOU AWAKE AT NIGHT?

# Chapter Ten

## Internet Research & The 21ˢᵗ Century Bathroom Wall

Without a doubt, the thing that leads so many people down the wrong road is what I would characterize as *"online research."* Be careful whenever you decide to wade waist deep in the online cesspool of deception, misinformation and opinion. Real research requires more than A simple 5 minute google search. I have a young client named Stephen whom had managed to get himself caught up in confusion and frustration after spending a few minutes online. By the way, minutes he'll never get back! I wasn't totally shocked because Stephen was from a generation who grew up online. I suppose to him, the online search felt comfortable and normal. One day, in a small panic, he came to see me with confusion hanging over him like a dark cloud. He told me that I should look at the links that he emailed me prior to our meeting. As expected, he had 5 or 6 links from what appeared to be *"credible sources"* all with conflicting viewpoints. One by one we went through each post and I showed him who or what was behind them. Every link to every post was carefully placed by an individual or company with something to sell or something to gain. Once we had discussed the questions that were plaguing him and he was comfortable and satisfied, we then proceeded with his plan. His online research may have cost him time and confusion but in the end, he made the right decision; a decision that will provide him with confidence and a strategy.

About a year later Stephen paid me another visit. This time we were having our annual review. He told me towards the end that he was grateful to me for helping to clear up his confusion about what he was originally reading online. I leaned in and said, *"Stephen, I know your generation thinks that the information superhighway started during your watch but actually it's been around a lot longer than you might think. The information superhighway dates-back to a time before my father was born."* Stephen looked at me in mild astonishment. I went on to say that *"prior to personal computers being in every home, people back in those earlier times could attain the very same sort of information by simply*

WHAT KEEPS YOU AWAKE AT NIGHT?

*visiting a local public restroom stall. There you could usually count on much of the same information and maybe more.*" The point is that you cannot believe every post, blog or website that you stumble upon online. The internet simply allows many of the same old opinions and agendas to reach a wider audience. Magic markers have now been replaced by a mouse and keyboard and **The Internet Has Become The New Bathroom Wall.**

## What Will Be Your Legacy in a Hundred Years?

Visualize forward about a hundred years or so to a generation that shares your last name. *Can you picture it?* A beautiful home in a nice neighborhood. Kids and puppies playing in the yard. As you enter the front door you are greeted by the warmth of a fireplace. Over the mantle there is a portrait, *but you just cannot make it out clearly.* Let me stop you right there at that point and allow me to pose a question. **What will be your Legacy in a Hundred Years and Beyond?** Most families have someone who began the family legacy. The person credited with starting the family legacy is usually the person in the portrait over the fireplace years and years later. Your portrait and mementoes of your life will likely be either prominently displayed or packed up in a box in the attic. You may be of a different opinion and that is okay. You may believe that as a favorite aunt or uncle or other family member that you are forever in the hearts and thoughts of future generations. Favorites typically last for a generation, maybe two. The Family Legacy Founder is remembered and spoken fondly of centuries later. **So, what would you like your Legacy to look like? Will it be your portrait displayed for all to see?**

## Final Comments

It has been my intent from the moment that I decided to write this book to bring honesty, clarity, wisdom, insight and even some bits of humor to a subject that most people try to avoid until it's too late to change game-plans. I sincerely hope that you the reader, learned a few new things and that you feel comfortable challenging the status quo. Never forget, **You Do Not Need to Risk Your Financial Future To Achieve Your Goals.**

WHAT KEEPS YOU AWAKE AT NIGHT?

# The Future Is Yours!

For more information or to schedule a no cost, no obligation analysis contact **Hurricane Financial Corp. at (888) 200-8161** or simply email us at Info@HurricaneFinancial.com

You can visit our website at HurricaneFinancial.com to request an appointment.

Initial meetings with people who are out of state will take place through an online video meeting link.

## Hurricane Financial Corp.

*Wealth.   Security.   Control.    In The Eye of The Storm!*

WHAT KEEPS YOU AWAKE AT NIGHT?

**116**

WHAT KEEPS YOU AWAKE AT NIGHT?

# Testimonials, Opinions and Thoughts

I have known Mr. Frank Riedel for almost eight years. It has truly been my pleasure working with and learning from Frank, He is Truly One in a Million. I've had a front row seat to witness his work with many of my clients and friends. Financial decisions can prove to be quite the daunting task, most people don't know where to start or what questions to even ask. Frank does a remarkable job of connecting the dots. His knowledge is vast and his ability to convey it to the client in a language they can understand is impressive. If your somebody, looking for honest financial advice, look no further.

Bruce Stedwell
Greeley, Co

I found Hurricane Financial after a long exhausting search that took over 6 months. My search encompassed multiple books and countless conversations with multiple advisors. The success of my family financial system hinged on creating a strong and solid foundation. I was referred directly to Mr. Frank Riedel from a trusted, reputable source. Mr. Riedel's expertise was easily apparent, and he proved to us again and again that we had finally found the right advisor for our needs. The strategy that was designed for us is a complete Godsend. We now have assets growing in a safe environment and high cash build up's for future investment needs.

My wife and I feel blessed to have Hurricane Financial and Mr. Riedel as a core part of our family financial system. We have already begun to refer Mr. Riedel to our friends, family and colleagues and will continue to do. I would recommend to anyone to take time to meet with Mr. Riedel and benefit from his great skill level and experience.

Ehimemen O Iboaya, MD.
Hillsborough, NC.

# Testimonials, Opinions and Thoughts

With a fresh marriage and an infant son, I made the decision to leave behind the stability of a job as a municipal firefighter/paramedic to pursue a new career in physical therapy, with the ultimate goal of opening a private practice. While I planned for my family's financial wellbeing across the transition, a trusted friend directed me to Frank Riedel at Hurricane Financial Corp. I am grateful for the referral! I was impressed by Frank's knowledge and customer service, The HFC staff was also very helpful. Angela's creativity, and HFC's commitment to my financial security and flexibility. HFC designed several unique insurance policies that will provide for my family in the event of my death. They also provide us with peace of mind while I'm alive. Perhaps most importantly, the instruments have been structured to facilitate financial autonomy. I have leveraged my policies to optimize cash flow during graduate school, finance the down payment for our home, and cover essential start-up expenses for my physical therapy practice. I can't imagine navigating these life events without the tools, expertise, and support I found through HFC. I am so pleased with the experience of working with Hurricane Financial and recommend them to friends, family, colleagues, and anyone else looking to optimize financial health and wealth.

Dave Bond, PT, DPT
Physical Therapist and Owner of Tōnn Physio, PLLC Bellingham, Washington


I had my 401k invested and managed by a large investment company. They made more money than I did. A friend told me about Hurricane Financial and my husband and I are glad we set up an appointment. Thank you, Mr. Riedel for the time that you and your staff spent helping us. My husband and I am now finally able to look forward to enjoying our retirement and being able to travel. Thanks again HFC.


Peggy Sommers
Greeley, CO.

WHAT KEEPS YOU AWAKE AT NIGHT?

# Testimonials, Opinions and Thoughts

I've had the privilege to know Frank Riedel and to call him my friend for over 10 years. What Frank writes in this book is not just hearsay, it is valuable information based upon his own personal experiences of tragedy to triumph in his own personal life. Today, Frank uses that real-life experience to help others to make good financial decisions. Congratulations Frank on a job well done!

Michael Todd Avery
Investment Advisor
Representative
Lexington, KY.

My Experience with Hurricane Financial was great. I was very impressed with the professionalism and the promptness of the process. I felt very comfortable making the decision with the advice given. It felt like a family member giving me advice.
Thank you for everything.

Nizar Noureddine, MD.

Frank has been a constant in our lives for over a decade. Our family has relied on his professional advice. He proves to be an expert time and again. Frank is a professional in every way who enjoys getting to know his clients personally too. Frank isn't just an advisor to us. We consider him a personal friend as well.

Dugan Prater
Birmingham, AL.

# Testimonials, Opinions and Thoughts

The financial industry can be so paralyzing to people. Often times, it is presented to people outside the industry through the lens of fear. Complexity and fear lead to bad decision making, and to make matters worse, these days financial advisors are not typically the most trusted group of people. Frank Riedel separates himself through 2 simple ways. First, he does what he says he will do. Secondly, Frank has the ability to take very complex strategies, and communicate them in ways that empower people to make great decisions. Frank is a coach, and I am glad that he has finally taken his insights and put them into this book for people to use as a road map to financial success.

Unlike many authors, Frank is actually, out working with clients every day. Additionally, he "eats his own cooking," which means that he is willing to put his money where his mouth is with his own family's retirement strategy! He practices what he preaches.

Justin Ross, Founder and Owner, YOUnify Consulting

After a long career in the Oil & Gas Industry, I was ready to retire. However, I was confused and honestly a bit nervous after talking to various investment company's and advisors. After hearing what they could offer and weighing their management fees, I found myself more unsure. Their comments about my scenario had me very worried as to whether or not I had saved enough in my 401k and pension account to retire. I eventually met with Frank Riedel at Hurricane Financial. Finally, I found someone who listened to my concerns and helped to put together a long-term plan. Now that I am fully retired. This plan has given me great peace mind. I am thankful to Mr. Riedel and his team at Hurricane Financial. They are Honest and always respectful. I have recommended HFC to a number of my friends and previous coworkers and will continue to do so.

Tim H.
Greeley, CO.

# Testimonials, Opinions and Thoughts

I had a 401k that we were unsure how to plan out our Retirement. We were introduced to Mr. Frank Riedel at HFC. Mr. Riedel helped us to put together a complete plan for our retirement years. We really appreciate the clear honesty and professionalism. My wife and I both wish we had met Mr. Riedel earlier in life. However, today we now sleep better at night. Thank you for helping my wife and I secure our financial future.

Rick Buckley
Loveland, CO.

I have been in law enforcement for nearly forty years. I will be retiring in less than two years. I started researching the best options for rolling over my police pension account. A friend suggested I contact Hurricane Financial. I was extremely impressed with their knowledge and ability to develop a long-term strategy. Hurricane Financial eased the burden and anxiety that comes with financial planning. I feel much more confident that my retirement savings is secure. The staff at Hurricane Financial was friendly, professional and a pleasure to work with. I highly recommend Hurricane Financial to anyone who is in the process of planning for retirement.

James R.
Sergeant
Greeley, Colorado

WHAT KEEPS YOU AWAKE AT NIGHT?

# Testimonials, Opinions and Thoughts

Intrigued by the Infinite Banking Concept (IBC), I read every book, blog, and website I could find, and, throughout my research, one critical concept became apparent. FIND THE RIGHT AGENT TO HELP YOU THROUGH THE PROCESS OR YOU MIGHT END UP IN A DISASTER! After creating my first IBC package with the help of the Frank Riedel team, I can rest assured that I was in good hands. Mr. Riedel, through multiple video conferences, stepped me through the entire process and carefully explained the theories, requirements, and possible outcomes for each policy I considered. Meeting with me later in the evening and even on Saturdays, I felt the strong, personalized commitment that I have yet to experience with any other brokerage or financial advisor. Moving forward with building and applying for my policy, Frank recommended an excellent insurance company with an established track record. They kept in constant contact and helped me complete all the prerequisites quickly and accurately. In the end, I came away with exactly what I wanted, a stable, affordable IBC investment product, MEC line safe, for years to come. If you're considering the IBC or are even ready to move forward with your investment, I strongly recommend Frank Riedel and staff.

Michael Barna, MD, MPH
Jacksonville, NC

# Testimonials, Opinions and Thoughts

Frank is someone that you find yourself thanking the Lord that you have him in your life. It is often said among Frank's peers how grateful you are to have him in your corner in life. Frank is a man of Integrity and a person that I have had the honor of watching him live his life out well. His expertise and knowledge base give him the ability to serve people at an incredibly high level.

Bill Walton
Founder, Accelerated Consulting and Management
Puerto Rico

Over the past 12 plus years Mr. Riedel and I have worked closely on several industry related projects. I have always been Impressed with Frank's Integrity and Vision. Frank is a tireless worker and always strives to serve his clientele with very best. I am reminded of this every time I meet with other advisors. The difference between Frank and most other advisors is like day and night. Frank is without question one of the very best advisors in the United States. I can recommend him without any hesitation to anyone whom is looking for Integrity and Clear, Honest Advice without any hidden agendas.

Robert Newhart JR
North Carolina

# Testimonials, Opinions and Thoughts

My experience with Hurricane Financial has been great. Thank you, Mr. Riedel and HFC for helping to explain options for our retirement nest-egg. Thank you also for never pressuring us to do anything and counseling us as to how best position our assets.

Randy B.
Colorado

**125**
WHAT KEEPS YOU AWAKE AT NIGHT?

**126**
WHAT KEEPS YOU AWAKE AT NIGHT?

**127**
WHAT KEEPS YOU AWAKE AT NIGHT?

Made in the USA
Columbia, SC
10 September 2025

61966432R00070